WHAT'S WRONG WITH
FORMALIZATION
– IN ECONOMICS ? –

An Epistemological
Critique

Henry K. H. Woo

Victoria Press
39865, Cedar Blvd., Suite 240
Newark, CA 94560, U.S.A.

Rm. 202, Hung On Mansion
177-181 Jaffe Road,
Hong Kong

Library of Congress Cataloging-in-Publication Data
Woo, Henry, K. H., 1946-
    What's wrong with formalization in economics?

    Bibliography: p.
    Includes index.
    1. Economics — Methodology.   2. Economics, Mathematical.   I. Title.
HB131.W66   1985   330'.01   85-22783
ISBN 0-9613204-2-7 (pbk.)

First published 1986
Printed in Hong Kong

CONTENTS

Acknowledgements

I would like, first of all, to thank my associates at the Hong Kong Institute of Economic Science for their kindest help and encouragement throughout the project. In particular I am deeply indebted to Rex Li for his dedicated and excellent editing work and his substantial contribution towards Chapter Five of the book. To P.C. Lund, I owe another great debt of gratitude. His many discussions with me and his valuable suggestion for rewriting, in particular in respect of Chapters Two and Three, have been extremely helpful.

At various stages in the progress of this work, I received comments, suggestions or materials from many people. I would like to thank all of them: Maurice Allais, Jack J. Bame, Peter T. Bauer, Mark Blaug, W.A. Brock, Bruce J. Caldwell, David C. Colander, Raymond Courbis, Béla Csikós-Nagy, Gerard Debreu, Sheila C. Dow, Amitai Etzioni, Edwin J. Feulner, Jr., John R. Fisher, Daniel R. Fusfeld, Donald R. Gentner, John Hicks, Homa Katouzian, Charles P. Kindleberger, Jürgen Kuczynski, Frederic S. Lee, Wassily Leontief, S.C. Littlechild, Donald McCloskey, Eugene J. Meehan, Ezra Mishan, Basil J. Moore, Laurence S. Moss, Alec Nove, Luigi Pasinetti, William H. Peterson, Claude Ponsard, Robert B. Reich, David Rumelhart, Jonas Salk, Warren J. Samuels, Theodore W. Schultz, G.L.S. Shackle, Martin Shubik, Ota Sik, Herbert A. Simon, Paul M. Sweezy, Pedro C.M. Teichert, Lester C. Thurow, Jan Tinbergen, Andrew Tylecote, David Warsh, E. Roy Weintraub, Bruce J. West; as well as members of the Institute for Socioeconomic Studies at New York. I would like, in particular, to thank the following people for their exceptionally thorough-going criticisms and important editorial improvements to the book: Peter Earl, William Frazer, K.K. Fung, Henri Guitton, Jack Wiseman.

To my secretary, Linda Lee, I must express my deep appreciation for her typing of innumerable drafts of the work. Finally, I would like to register my thanks to Pauline Ho and Ken Ho for their attending to miscellaneous matters related to the work.

January 1986, Hong Kong.   HENRY K.H. WOO

Chapter One
The Advent of Wholesale
Formalism in Economics

The Advent of Wholesale Formalism

No serious economist is against the application of mathematical and formalization[1] techniques to economics.[2] What causes concern over present-day economics is the dominance of mathematics to the almost exclusion of other methods of enquiry and the subsequent imposition of a mathematical finality on the subject. This is abundantly clear as one scans major academic journals in the profession. Alternatively put, the problem is not that mathematical techniques are being put to use to solve specific problems, where appropriate, but that mathematicization has practically become the total approach in economic analysis governing the intellectual content and output of the entire discipline. Indeed, mathematicization in economics has developed to the point where it appears that only economic knowledge in the mathematical form or translatable into the mathematical form constitutes significant and therefore respectable economic knowledge.[3]

How all this started and developed has always been a most interesting question. There is no lack of studies analyzing the sociology of this phenomenon.[4] Equally interesting are the explicit concerns expressed over the impact of such *"wholesale formalism"* on economics by its leading practitioners. Significant as these enquiries and concerns were, the present author believes that the fundamental problems of the issue, namely, the relative significance of formalization in economics from the broader perspective of what formalization can or cannot contribute towards what we expect of progress in economic knowledge, the relative strength and weakness of formalization as compared to other modes of enquiry, etc. remain largely unexplored. It is hoped that answers to these fundamental questions can throw light on the limits and limitations of formalization, and with them, the key issue of the potential contributions of formalization versus those of other modes of enquiry could be clarified.

The Merits of Formalization

It would be a useful starting point to first summarize the merits of formalization and how mathematical economists build upon such strengths. Suppes (1968, pp.654-58) for instance specifically sees formalization as having the following philosophical payoffs: (1) formalizing a connected family of concepts is one way to bring out their meaning in an explicit fashion; (2) formalization results in the standardization of terminology and the methods of conceptual analysis for various branches of sciences; (3) the generality provided by formalization enables us to determine the essential features of theories; (4) formalization provides a degree of objectivity which is otherwise impossible to achieve; (5) formalization makes clear exactly what is being assumed, and thus is a safeguard against ad hoc and post hoc verbalizations; (6) formalization enables one to determine what the minimal assumptions are which a theory requires.[5]

Of central importance, too, is the fact that the formal machinery enables us to handle studies with a high degree of technical complexity. This is possible because within a formal system, definitional and substitutional procedures can be employed whereby we can compress without limit complex formulae into simpler forms. Since the formalized formula permits easier computerization, it lends convenience to empirical verification and testing at least in a nominal sense. With further aid from the computer, formalization enables us to tackle problems and puzzles of immense complexity, far exceeding what our attention span of particular notions and their interrelations can handle. As a corollary, formalization enables the theorist to draw the most hidden of conclusions that are unobvious to the "mind's eye." It is, so to speak, capable of "fine-tuning" analytic results of a given set of fundamental premises to the finest possible degree.

Lest it is taken for granted that axiomatic systems have only a static and expository role, Granger argues further that axiomatization, effective and justified from the outset of research, is the instrument of discovering and testing. Contributing to the destruction of the prejudices of evidence and the sharpening of the relations between symbolism and experience, it helps in the case of human sciences to rectify embryonic scientific thought, which "is too easily blinded and confused by the brightness and glitter of experienced meanings" (Granger, 1983, p.137).

Each of the above claims is by itself desirable enough. Should these claims be truly substantiated, these qualities in combination enable the formal machinery to wield formidable power, permitting its application to almost any conceivable subject or situation. It is not surprising, therefore, that the common preoccupation of professional economists has become one of merely asking how good a formalization is or can be. Whether or not a subject or a situation is formalizable or whether it should be formalized is never a question of concern. With such formidable power in command by the formal machinery, little wonder even the most moderate and enlightened of economists can only plead that non-mathematical approaches should not be discriminated against and warn against the excessive and indiscriminate application of mathematics.[6] The power of mathematicization as found in economics to date, it seems, is almost absolute and wholly taken for granted by the majority of the profession.

The Minority View

There is, however, a minority group of economists, including some leading economists, who see the detrimental impacts of wholesale mathematicalism and who have all along been attacking it from different directions. One conventional attack is that lopsided emphasis on mathematical techniques leads unavoidably to the undesirable development where the form dictates the content of enquiry and where the availability of certain techniques determines the choice of problems. It is natural that a particular set of techniques for academic enquiry is more amenable to certain types of content. In the case of mathematicization in economics, it seems to have developed to the point where real problems which are not readily amenable to mathematical manipulation are being ignored. As a corollary, this has in turn led to lopsided emphasis on those areas or "puzzles" which happen to be easily manipulatable by mathematical techniques. The elevation of technique above substance and form above content have contributed pervasively to inappropriate practices and habits of mind. It leads to preoccupation with economic phenomena and features which can genuinely or spuriously be quantified, the consequent neglect of those which cannot be so treated but are frequently more germane, as well as the neglect of the historical and institutional background (Bauer, 1981, p.265).

Another line of attack is related to the interpretation of analytic results of formal operations. Economists are charged with the neglect of interpreting in the non-formal language the significance of their theorems, i.e., their relevance to the real world, and the range of values of their variables within which they are valid. Indeed many economists have been in the habit of just producing a formal model, taking it as perfectly legitimate to leave the model to others to work out the mapping to reality. Such loosely interpreted results, as Meehan (1982) pointed out, render most of them useless for policy-making. For a mathematical model to represent the real world, it is of paramount importance that the formal concepts and the syntactical relations between these concepts are mappable onto the real world articulated in the pre-formalized language. Also of equal importance is the appraisal, inevitable in the non-formal language, of what part or aspect of reality has or has not been captured by the formalization and the relation between what has been captured and what has been left out by the formalization. Otherwise such formalizations would be dissociated from reality and might be of zero or even negative contribution to economic knowledge. The burden of decoding the formal language, it should be obvious, rests with the theorizing economist if mathematicization were to realize its intended use.

These attacks, however, in no way relegate the presumed significance of mathematicization. All that is really needed, it appears, is for mathematical economists to exercise prudence and to enhance their sense of self-discipline in the application of their mathematical techniques. It is therefore largely a question of attitude and awareness of the practising profession, and this should in no way affect the real contribution of formalization.

The Controversy of Unreal Assumptions

There is, however, a more piercing criticism from the non-mathematical economist, namely, most of the axioms of formal economic models are unreal. This has to be the case since mathematicization dictates some kind of amenability of these axioms to formulation in the abstract mathematical language and thus serious distortion of the economic reality is unavoidable. Formalization thus leads to the creation of an unreal economics.[7]

To this, the mathematical economist can retort that any representation of the real world by the human language requires some degree of abstraction, and conversely some distortion of reality. What is important is not that the axioms distort reality, which they necessarily do, but that the distortion is consistent throughout the whole formalization, and that the distortion is taken into account in the final interpretation of the theorems derived. In other words, the real question is whether or not the distortion is "containable." Since the formal machinery is content-neutral, it can be expected that the distortion is faithfully and neutrally transmitted to the theorems. As a result, whether the axioms distort reality is only a matter of degree, and would not be affected by the formal rules chosen. Indeed Friedman (1953, p.14) has gone even as far as claiming that "to be important, a hypothesis must be descriptively false in its assumptions." What matters is the predictive accuracy of the propositions derived from the set of axioms postulated. As long as the predictive results are true of the real world, distortion in the basic premises is immaterial.

Against this position, critics of the "unreal" assumptions take on another line of argumentation. Hutchison (1977, p.89), for instance, interprets the prevailing situation as a crisis of abstraction. He argues that although "some degree of abstraction is essential and inevitable in virtually any kind of scientific study, it seems to be presumed that no degree or kind of abstraction needs any defence or explanation; as regards abstract assumptions, anything goes: it's simply a matter of 'temperament' and there is no epistemological price to be paid." In other words, what he is against is the wild excesses and the ill-disciplined manner in the kind of abstractions pursued within the economics profession, abstractions that do not seem to measure up to its traditional aims and claims. This situation is similarly and widely deplored by other leaders in the profession. Boulding (1966), Frisch (1970), Leontief (1971), Worswick (1972), Phelps Brown (1973), on different occasions have sounded out warnings against such excesses. Unfortunately "excesses" thus broadly conceived is difficult to appraise unless they come down to specifics, and by the time a specific situation comes to be assessed, it turns out that it can be subject to a variety of interpretations.

Interesting too, are the criticisms raised by the Austrian School. Mises, for instance, is well-known in opposing the idea of using mathematics in economics. To him, "the problems of process analysis, i.e., the only economic problems that matter, defy any mathematical approach." (Mises, 1966, p.356). Hayek, too, pointed out that considering only theories that include measurable variables has the consequence of overlooking the "true" theory. Unlike the position that exists in the physical sciences, in economics and other disciplines that deal with essentially complex phenomena, the aspects of the events to be accounted for about which we can get quantitative data are necessarily limited and may not include the important ones (1978, p.24). In a like-minded vein Shackle (1972) also pointed out that mathematics can only explore what is already given. We cannot claim knowledge so long as we acknowledge novelty.

The Counter-Offensive of the Mathematical Economists

While these criticisms or warnings have largely fallen on deaf ears, in particular among economists of the younger generation who are brought up in the tradition of mathematical economics, it is not the case that mathematical economists of important stature have ignored such criticisms.[8] Indeed, within the camp of mathematical economics, a lot of exciting work has been going on both to deliver an answer to these criticisms and to consolidate their apparent gains so "solidly" made.

One direction of research is that of replacing overtly unreal assumptions with more realistic ones within the framework of the general equilibrium theory. Dynamic equilibrium models are built to relax the stationarity of conventional equilibrium theory. Assumptions about perfect divisibility, the continuity of variables, convexity of production and consumption sets, concavity of preference functions, etc. are cautiously being relaxed to provide modified formulations of the general equilibrium framework. Most of these attempts, however, are unable to go very far since the modifications are made largely in the "non-sensitive areas" (Kornai, 1971).

More radical proposals and efforts in the same direction are not lacking. Kornai (1971), for instance, advocates the adoption of "axioms of more general force," axioms which are more realistic than those of the general equilibrium school, concepts such as pressure and suction, conflict and compromise, etc. Allias (1977), for instance, has been laboring to replace what he calls the "monist market economy model" by his "pluralist model of the economy of markets," which in his mind, preserves the essential features of reality, without being subordinated to any restrictive assumptions about continuity, differentiability of functions or convexity.

Impressive achievements are made, too, in the area of bringing in new and more sophisticated mathematical techniques into economic analysis. Topological mathematics, non-standard analysis, optimal control theory, cybernetics, the systems approach, fuzzy set theory,[9] etc. are introduced into economics to provide formal representation of the complexities and hierarchical interconnections of economic organizations and systems, as well as to accommodate as much as possible the differentiations of individual behaviors and actions. Increasingly it is being held that the injection of more sophisticated mathematical techniques will improve our capability of representing higher degrees of complexity and differentiations in reality, in spite of and regardless of fundamental problems confronting the very foundations of mathematics (Kline, 1980, p.275-76). Katzner (1983), for instance, has shown that to make inferences about equilibria, causality, or dynamics, etc., it is not necessary for the variables concerned to be measurable, and thereby expressible in real numbers. Mathematically, we can analyze such properties even if we cannot measure the concepts in question. We can, say, ask whether there exists an equilibrium level of modernization even if we cannot measure modernization. It is therefore possible that, with ingenuity and care, we will be able in principle, to construct formal economic models approaching analogue with reality[10] and to draw the most subtle of conclusions out of them.

Behind this conviction lies a "progressivist" philosophy of formalization espoused by those outstanding masters in mathematical economics such as Neumann and Morgenstern (1944) and shared by most mathematical economists. The reasons why mathematical treatment of economics does not appear to be fruitful, if this were the case at all, lie in that the development of descriptive economics has not reached a stage of maturity for mathematicization and in that we have not yet created the right mathematics to treat economic behavior. We can, however, expect gradual but orderly improvements over time, if economists "take up first problems contained in the very simplest facts of economic life and try to establish theories which explain them and which really conform to rigorous scientific standards. We can have enough confidence that from then on the science of economics will grow further, gradually comprising matters of more vital importance than those with which one has to begin" (p.7). In the same enthusiastic spirit, Koopmans (1957, p.177) talked of a convergence of "mathematical" and "literary" economics "The welcome result is that 'mathematical' and 'literary' economics are moving closer to each other. They meet on the ground of a common requirement for good hard thought from explicit basic postulates, rather than for manipulative skills in calculus, differential equations, or determinants. To illustrate: in some intuitive sense the 'distance' between A. P. Lerner's *The Economics of Control* and the mathematical formulations of the propositions of welfare economics reviewed in the first essay of this book *(i.e. Koopmans,1957)* is, I believe, not large. If there is a difference, it is one of succinctness of expression rather than of content, concepts, or objective."

But is this really the case? Is this possibility for a theory to eventually reach a state of analogue with reality something that is inherent in the very potentials of formalization? Can we in any way justify the tacit claim behind this position, namely, that for any aspect of reality, already realized or to be anticipated, there must exist or will surely evolve in the realm of mathematics a specific set of techniques that can create a representation in full analogue with this particular aspect of reality? And if this position is not justifiable *a priori,* can we justify it in any other reasonable way?

Are Unreal Assumptions Acceptable?

Before we can answer these questions, it would be necessary and useful to examine the major question of making unreal assumptions in formalization. That is, are unreal assumptions, which constitute most of the axioms of our formal theories in economics, justifiable? The present author thinks that both proponents and critics in their simplistic ways of framing and handling the problem have not been able to deliver a decisive argument so far.[11]

It must be recognized that on the one hand, the very nature of representation of reality by symbols must entail some degree of "unrealness." Moreover, progress of knowledge would not have been possible if only propositions known to be real are accepted for theorization. Assumptions that are taken as unreal at a particular state of man's knowledge might turn out to be true of reality as his knowledge unfolds. There is thus a significant sense in which understanding always progresses by the entry of "unrealistic" assumptions.[12] But on the other hand, such "unrealness" cannot be taken as a *carte blanche* licence for defending any theory labelled as unreal.[13] Since the very process of abstraction, and by implication, theorization, constitutes the singling out of a finite set of features from the complexity and richness of reality, such abstraction means that all theories are inherently and necessarily incomplete. Framed in this manner, the question becomes one of how far, and under what conditions such incompleteness is acceptable, and what kind of incompleteness poses as obstacle to progress in our knowledge.

For such incompleteness to be acceptable, we might posit of a theory we advance that either what our theory singles out from the richness and complexity of reality are aspects relatively autonomous of those left out by the theory, or else we posit that from our theory, we could confidently expect that those omitted aspects of reality would be explicable or encompassable when our existing theory is expanded by addition of auxiliary but compatible hypotheses. If this set of criteria about the incompleteness of a theory cannot be met, then a theory that distorts reality would be an unacceptably "false" theory. In other words, there is a special kind of incompleteness about it that is not acceptable. On the contrary, if the incompleteness presents a reasonable prospect of being a stepping stone towards more comprehensive truth or does not deter the realization of these steps, we can tentatively presume that the theory, as far as its distortion of reality goes, is acceptable. Conversely, if such an incompleteness fails to meet these criteria, then the way reality is distorted by that theory is deemed unacceptable. The implication therefore is that we should develop more subtle criteria for evaluating the acceptability of the incompleteness of particular theories.

With this perspective in the background, we can see that the question of unrealness *per se* need not lend support to formalization nor does it constitute a decisive argument against formalization in economics, although it could be suspected that the formal method does not seem to possess the innate capability of preventing the adoption of unreal assumptions that are classified in the above as unacceptable. In this vein, the present author tends to believe that vigorous attempts made to sharpen or to innovate formal techniques in order to have more true-to-life representations, are mere efforts of well-intentioned economists trying to make up for the inherent weaknesses and limitations of formalization by their personal ingenuity. In subsequent chapters, it will be argued that searching formal representation of knowledge in the realm of social sciences could be a futile and risky business.

NOTES

1. "Formalization" is very often used interchangeably with "mathematicization" by the author though the former has a broader meaning. Throughout this work, this term is also used interchangeably in some instances with "axiomatization," though again it includes the latter in its meaning. Strictly speaking, formalization encompasses both the syntactical techniques of axiomatization and the semantic techniques of model theory.

2. Adopting this position amounts to "running counter to the principle of maximum efficiency" Géorgescu-Roegén (1971, p.331).

3. Cf. Katouzian (1980, p.57).

4. See, for instance, Homa Katouzian (1980, chap. 5).

5. The most successful examples of axiomatization come from physics, which include the axiomatizations of such theories as classical particle and rigid body mechanics, relativistic mechanics. Suppes (1968) has also pointed out that in a number of cases recourse to axiomatization in science has solved various conceptual problems or resolved various controversies. Some obvious examples are: Kolomogoror's axiomatization of probability which supplied the notion of probability with increased conceptual clarity, and Von Neumann's formalization of quantum theory which proved the equivalence of wave and matrix mechanics. Suppes also gives examples from physics and psycholinguistics where scientists, by not adhering to the rigor of axiomatization, have been led to make indefensible claims.

6. See, for example, Michio Morishima (1984). See also Homa Katouzian (1980).

7. John Blatt has, for instance, critically stated that what is practised in economics is "not the application of mathematics to the economic problems of the real world. Rather it is the application of highly precise and elaborate mathematics to an entirely imaginary and fanciful economic cloud cuckoo land." See Blatt (1983, p. 171).

8. Even Lawrence Klein, himself no mean exponent of the quantitative technique, criticized that mathematicization is becoming an end in itself, and abstruse mathematical models for models' sake are substituted for reflective thought.

9. The idea of a fuzzy set is still wholly arithmomorphic. Its ability to assign a number between 0 and 1 inclusive to all objects in the universe of discourse rests on the property of discrete distinctness of the elements involved.

10. According to Katzner, "all economic models may be regarded as arithmomorphic similes of underlying dialectical reality" (p. 140).

11. This, however, does not deny the contributions of Archibald (1959), Melitz (1965), Machlup (1978), etc. on this issue. For an up-to-date debate over the philosophical positions of scientific realism see Churchland and Hooker (1985).

12. I am indebted to Jack Wiseman for this point.

13. Friedman has in fact inverted Popper's falsification theory to defend unreal assumptions. While it is true that Popper analyzed empirical falsification to be the demarcating characteristic between science and non-science, Popper has made it perfectly clear that the purport of attempted falsification lies in thorough-going criticism that we can and should adopt to criticize and thereby evaluate a theory. Friedman has inverted this idea of falsification into a "criticism-barring" strategy by asserting that all other types of criticisms can be ignored as long as one type of criticism — i.e. attempted falsification by the intended predictive consequences of a theory — can be met!

Chapter Two
The Paradox of Abstraction
in Social Sciences

Qualitative vs Quantitative Distortion of Reality

With the phenomenal development of mathematical techniques and their wide-ranging application to economics, it appears that the vision and contribution of the mathematical economists are in their firm grip. The question, it seems, is merely one of whether or not the present rate and the magnitude of progress can be further sustained. Such optimism, however, is pre-maturely founded.

We take it that a piece of formalization is useful if it is capable of meeting the following criteria. First, we have to ask whether or not it is capable of picking from the stock of the pre-formalized concepts and relations for formalization those aspects that reflect some essential properties in reality. Second, we have to determine whether or not the syntactical relations built into the formalized concepts in the formalization do correspond with some structural relations in reality. Third, we have to tell whether these relations and properties singled out for formalization are fairly autonomous of other non-formalized relations or properties such that they can be taken as independently workable hypotheses. The validity of the above criteria is rather transparent, for it would be difficult to imagine any economist who would not like to claim living up to these standards as a merit for their formalization efforts.[1] However, what we need to be critical and vigilant about are the questions of first whether the formalization exercises in the social sciences are really capable of fulfilling such criteria and second whether economists have shown any effort in this direction in their eagerness to come up with impressive formalizations.

We may recall that some degree of distortion or even "falsification" of reality is necessary in any form of abstract reasoning. This arises from the fact that no man-made artifact or representational system can be in exact or complete analogue with reality, or made to generate a description of the world which matches it fully, point for point (Bronowski, 1966). It would indeed be inconceivable that man, a "rather" accidental product in the evolutionary process, could have come to possess the very perceptual and cognitive apparatus that can represent the world at once faithfully and comprehensively. This kind of structural dissonance between the properties of man as a knowing subject and those of reality as an object to be known entails that perfect congruence is unattainable. Given man's limited representational resources in contrast to the supposedly infinitely intricate and deep reality which is to be represented, abstraction and economy of expression are what we need to make a virtue out of necessity. As a result, generalization devices or approximation schemata have to be employed in human cognition to subsume events, entities or phenomena which are rather uniform or identical. If one were sufficiently observant and sensitive, reality is always richer in qualities, in hints and symptoms for further underlying mechanisms and related factors, than what is encapsulated in formulated theories, let alone formalized ones. In other words, all theories represent just a selection of possible systematic factors which could be singled out as salient and that there are always indications of further and deeper content to even that circumscribed part of reality we intend our theories to encapsulate. Hence any abstraction or abstract reasoning implies inescapably some degree of distortion of reality.[2]

The Meta-Structure of Physical and Human Reality

In the physical realm, atomic units that constitute or contribute to a phenomenon can be considered largely uniform or near-uniform, thereby capable of being subsumed, for theorizing purposes, under well-chosen variables. As a result, they are amenable to representation and manipulation by various types of mathematical structures built invariably upon basic logical connectives, i.e., "and" and "or" which postulate *extensional* states of conjunction and disjunction as well as "it is not the case that," which postulates the strictly exclusive state of negation. Partly as a result of its atomic elements, the causal structure of the physical reality is often so stable that for all intents and purposes, causal relations between such elements can be represented in a formal deductive framework founded upon the notion of material implication, i.e., "if". Protons, for instance, is believed to have such a longevity of say, at least ten thousand billion billion billion years that it is not necessary to take into account its possible decay into positrons for most purposes. As a result, any formal deductive system employing the notions of "if", "and", "or" etc. can be expected to map fairly well the *meta-structure of the physical reality*. What remains to be filled in would be specific contents, e.g., variables and laws governing their specific relations. Thus, we usually find an adequate analogue between the formal machinery and the physical phenomenon under study. The adequacy of this analogue constitutes, in other words, the necessary and sufficient condition for a valid piece of formalization. As a result, such distortions that we have described in the previous paragraph do not as a rule present much problem.[3] The distortions in most cases are essentially "quantitative" in nature. A graph plotted to join some data points may not be a perfect fit and an observed magnitude may vary within some acceptable limits around the values predicted by the theory. But on the whole, it is still the case that until a better theory arises, an existing formula poses no problem of distortion. At the least, it constitutes the best approximation so far of the data giving the various values of measured magnitudes.

By contrast, the meta-structure of the human reality is such that social and economic phenomena are much less containable within the logico-mathematical structures that are hinged on extensional conceptions of "andness" and "or-ness", etc. Individual human agents who constitute or contribute to human phenomena cannot be presumed to be uniform, or anything near uniform, except perhaps in very primitive societies or economies back in history prior to the development of self-consciousness.[4] In modern societies, individuals with their particular personal history or personality etc. are far-from-uniform. As a result, a large part of social and economic phenomena that result from the collective actions of such far-from-uniform agents are expectedly characterized by "far-from-equilibrium states"[5] and are inherently unstable. The causal relations between these states and phenomena can be loose, mutually interactive or even retro-active. They are much too fuzzy and individuated to map into formal deductive representations relying upon sweeping extensional notions of logical implication, conjunction or negation. As a consequence, distortions of reality in economics or other social sciences are very different in nature and are much less containable or tractable than the distortions in the physical sciences. They are more outright distortions that we cannot easily track down, evaluate their consequences, translate and make allowance for.[6] The case of distortion in economics and in the social sciences we can call "qualitative distortion." By this we refer to cases where a particular formula contains concepts or variables, e.g., capital or labor, that encompass or subsume qualitatively different instances or variations which are not inter-substitutable over a wide range of cases. It is obvious and often rightly taken for granted that, when we deal with physical phenomena, the mathematical relations between the values of the variables in a formula can be treated as a theory postulating systematically the relations between the dependent and independent variables by which reality is depicted. In other words, we can expect that for each and every particular case where the formula is supposed to apply, the values of the variables in question can change within the entire prescribed ranges of these variables without disrupting the relations between these variables.

Mathematical Relations as Surface Labels

But such constancy of the theorized relations between variables — amidst changes in the values of variables within the entire prescribed range — is often not found in the social reality supposedly depicted by mathematical formulae in the social sciences. A formula might appear to be applicable to a wide range of particular cases, but when the values of the variables change beyond fairly narrow ranges in a particular case, either the prescribed relation may no longer hold, or even more drastically, that particular phenomenon or entity may cease to exist altogether. For this reason, that formula cannot be regarded as a theory about the reality being referred to. It is just a surface indicator or label, and a very misleading one for that matter, for the label usually conceals far more complexity in reality than that it alerts us to.

Take the production function for example. If we take each production unit that has already been formed for one reason or another, then it can be said that capital and labor contributed towards production. But whatever mathematical relation that is employed in the production function, be it additive, multiplicatory, etc. is incapable itself of encompassing a theory in the true sense of the word in that it can explicate the relation between the particular capital and particular labor in each particular production unit in reality. The labor has to possess the right kind of skill and to be motivated and disciplined in the right manner to fit in with the capital available. The capital has to be in the right mix of cash, real estate, machinery, copy-right, etc. The two have to match each other and often have to evolve alongside with each other before they can work together to result in production of the right goods and services. Given an existing production unit, there is only a very limited range within which capital and labor can be substituted.

Very often, changes or substitutions beyond that narrow range would be counter-productive or even result in the breakdown of the production unit. Mere difference in scale, for instance, can sometimes entail that the entity or phenomenon being referred to by the formula falls into a different category with qualitatively different relations. One firm with a capital stock say twenty times larger than another in the same trade does not (and usually cannot) differ from the other merely in the size of output. It might also differ with respect to the technology employed, management style adopted, etc., leading to very different attitudes and corporate plans towards an existing market.

Thus, the mathematical relations between capital and labor in the production function serve at most as a crude and often obfuscating indicator of the rich and multifarious relations between the actual cases of capital and labor in reality. They are incapable of being used to theorize about the nature and range of the multifarious and intricate relations between capital and labor. A formula built upon such mathematical relations is unable even to acknowledge, let alone formulate, the restriction in substitution range within which the production function holds for a particular case, nor the necessary background conditions for the right mix and right relations between capital and labor to grow into the kind of production units we may find in reality at any one time. For another production unit, or type of production unit, there will be another type of restriction on inter-substitutability. The overall question that subsequently presents itself is whether or not we are capable of, and if so, how we go about exhausting such differentiations, which impose different inter-substitutability restrictions on different production enterprises, or different types of production enterprises. Even if we were able to list out and stipulate the restriction on substitution ranges, this listing exercise is not adequate for the understanding of the economic connections in question, for each substitution range discovered is merely the outward manifestation of the various qualitative relations that must hold in each particular case between the capital, labor and the nature of business of the enterprise.

In other words, the mathematical relation in this case is not adequate even to capture the phenomena, let alone the underlying factors giving rise to the phenomena. In the name of the commonplace defence that all theories, whether in mathematical form or not, must abstract from the richness of reality, it has often been forgotten that when a "theory" can be formulated only by ignoring the substitution restrictions among values of its variables and thereby their qualitative relations, what is postulated by such a "theory" would amount to an unjustifiable distortion of reality.

Such a "theory" would merely refer, in a very crude and misleading way, to some surface relations between variables while completely ignoring first the restrictions in inter-substitutability between values of variables and second the rich content behind the surface relations. Vary the values of the variable and the formula often breaks down. This means that part of the essential features in each particular case, i.e. the deeper intricate qualitative relations, has been systematically missed out by the mathematics. With this problem of qualitative distortion and subsumption, the most we can say for a formula is that when we apply it to a particular case, the formula would give us a static cross-section of that case at any one point in time. The choice of variables and of the relations stipulated between these variables would be completely uninformative about the conditions and processes by which such relations are generated, how they hold together, or how restricted is the range of values of the variables which can be substituted. In appearance, the formula may seem to be crudely true of some broader range of phenomena. But this would be the case only if the qualitative variations among the values of its variables are very limited and that the restrictions on the range of inter-substitutable values are few. And in the human world that is characterized largely by far-from-equilibrium states, it is inescapable that a large part of the concepts and variables we employ to theorize about the world are liable to subsume important qualitative variations. Some of these variations must be tolerated if we want to say anything to be of any significance, some are too fuzzy to articulate, and some have yet to be differentiated given the present state of our knowledge.

Law of Diminishing Field of Applicability

It may be said in defence that the mathematical economist who derives such a formula is not as naive as thus presumed. In the case of the production function, for instance, he may first make some preliminary assumptions about the input variables, namely, they are perfectly substitutable, they are subject to infinite divisibility, etc., so as to prescribe a valid universe of application for the production function in question. Such defence is, however, an obscurantist measure assuming away a host of fatal problems besetting the use of formalism. It obscures the boundary to the range within which the values of a variable can vary without leading to the breakdown of the formula. It obscures the question of what would be needed for the variables to interact and grow and form themselves before they develop into the kind of entity or phenomenon the formula refers to. It also obscures the need to differentiate cases arising from different inter-substitutability boundaries and inter-substitutability ranges.[7]

As the analysis of these issues is obscured by the very assumptions about the input variables, no systematically delineated range of "exceptions" can be read or inferred from the formalized theory itself. The economist is thereby forced to introduce indefinite series of exceptions occasioned by new instances popping up in reality in order to save a formula from being invalidated. In light of what are being obscured, there is also no easy way by which we can tell whether or not and under what conditions the domain of cases when the formula holds would be larger than the domain of exceptions. This possibility of indefinite, and probably even infinite, exceptional cases to a formula is liable to create the paradox that the more abstract a formula is, the more likely it would encompass qualitative variations among its variables that are not inter-substitutable. And bearing in mind the possible richness of exceptions, the more universal a formula appears, the more restricted its actual range of application is liable to be.

A similar paradox can also be drawn. The more sophisticated a formula is, i.e., the more sophisticated the postulated relations between its variables or the more the number of variables that are embedded within the formula, the more liable it will be to generate permutations of relations that subsume incommensurable variations. Such a formula is also less likely to be true of the real world. At the extreme, it simply becomes a special case in the infinitely many logical possibilities which are prohibitively difficult to be mapped onto the reality.

The above paradoxes are highly illuminating. They are pointing to the high likelihood of the existence of an inverse relation between the degree of abstraction and the sophistication of a formula in economics (or indeed in social sciences as a whole), and thereby its degree of subsumption of qualitative variations on the one hand, and its field of applicability on the other. A kind of law of diminishing field of applicability can thus be hypothesized, correlating inversely the extent of unqualified applicability of a formula to reality versus that formula's apparent universality and the apparent precision behind that universality. Qualified applicability of a formula to reality means a reduction in its empirical content. Hence, the empirical content of a formula is liable to decrease with an increase in the level of its abstraction or sophistication and also with an increase in the number of variables contained in it.

There is another significant aspect to the subsumption of qualitative variations, namely, the number of relevant ranges of inter-substitutable values delineated by factors governing a variable and the boundary of the range of inter-substitutable values to a variable cannot be taken as constant and in consequence cannot be assumed to remain unchanged over time. Consider again the case of the production function. To what extent capital and labor are inter-substitutable depends not only on the qualitative variations subsumed under these variables, but also very significantly on changes in those factors such as technology, organizational structure, management know-how, etc. Such interlocking relations and their essential openness can hardly be captured by joining together variables through syntactical relations offered by some formalization techniques.

It needs to be further pointed out that as a formula about the economic or social reality gets more complex, and thereby becoming less capable of explicating the complex relations and structures in reality, it reflects increasingly the syntactical properties of the very formal machinery from which it is derived. What we are looking at then is no longer the shape of reality as such, but the shape of the syntactical structure of that formula that has been trimmed of its range of applicability. In the extreme case, the formula is nothing more than a pure mathematical one exhibiting the properties of its syntactical system. It has become merely a game of refined expression using the techniques borrowed from logic and mathematics.

Thus in their enthusiasm to ape the physical sciences, social scientists have been oblivious of the above limitations in many of the mathematical formulae proffered for social science theories. In practice, it is often the case that the physical sciences have been studying phenomena uniform enough to be encapsulated by mathematical formulae without giving rise to qualitative distortions. On the other hand that part of reality studied by the social sciences is full of phenomena fuzzy enough to give rise to such distortions. Though there is no necessity that the physical reality should always be uniform enough to be encapsulated by mathematical formulae while the social reality should be in each and every case so fuzzy as to preclude the applicability of mathematical formulae to them, in theory as well as in practice, such is often the distinct difference between the physical and social parts of reality as studied by the physical and the social scientists.

The Indefensibility of Formalization in Social Science

To the above criticisms, the mathematical economist could have, however, a repertoire of replies. As has just been mentioned, he can argue that not all concepts in economics subsume qualitative variations to the same degree and not all qualitative variations subsumed give rise to the inter-substitutability problem. Some concepts, such as money and price, subsume less qualitative variations than, say, the concepts of capital and labor, and as a result, a formula incorporating the former is likely to be less curtailed in validity. This kind of exceptions can readily be admitted. Such differential in subsumption helps to explain why some economic phenomena are more amenable to mathematical treatment than others and for that matter yield more fruitful formalization results. Such amenability may also be true of those socio-economic environments which are simple, stagnant or relatively stable.[8] But the acceptance of this argument means that the scope of economics would be severely constricted, which no mathematical economist would like to see.

It might also be said that the mathematical economist can always improve his formal techniques in order to accommodate more flexibly certain modes of qualitative variations within his formulae, or he can even attempt to anticipate new variations yet to emerge. But this approach completely misses the whole point about the problem of qualitative distortion. Qualitative distortion is only a surface phenomenon given rise to by deeper and richer relations between the variables and could not be handled by the introduction of a more sophisticated formula. As has previously been pointed out, there is a kind of inverse relation between the sophistication of the theory and its likelihood of being removed from reality. The improvement of formal technique is thus more liable to lead the original theory away from reality than to capture the complexities in it.

The mathematical economist could also retort to the charge that mathematical formulae are mere surface labels of reality in the human world. It could, for instance, be argued that mathematical models can always be constructed upon the eventual discovery of causal relations between variables and that mathematics is neutral with respect to the nature of the variables, be they independent or dependent variables, static or dynamic variables, deep or surface variables, etc. Such an argument, however, misses the point that a social science variable, whatever specific classification it belongs to, tends to contain sub-variables, each of which in turn presupposes possibly a set of incommensurate though often interrelated factors at work. Arbitrary conjunction of these possibly different underlying mechanisms or factors into a single and simplistic logical schema under a mathematical formula can only confuse matter and is unlikely to represent faithfully the actual causal relations in reality. Even where some of such causal relations are capable of or eventually made ready for formal treatment, they are then most likely to be trivial and uninteresting ones. In other words, there is virtually little room for a "grand formalization" of social science theories of real significance.

When further refinement of formal techniques proves to be of no avail, and when a new sophisticated formula can only be of more restricted application, the mathematical economist might still argue that such formalization would have to be needed in the process of testing and refuting the theories behind the formal dress. Formalization, he would argue, is still the necessary tool to test effectively, if not conclusively, a theory in question.[9] But this is just forgetting the fact that the formalized theory has less content than its pre-formalized version. To check against error, it should be the more contentful version that should be brought to the test, and not the less contentful version alone. The mistake in theorization may lie in that part of the content missed out in the less contentful version. Thus, testing the less contentful version still leaves that part of the content of the pre-formalized theory trimmed for formalization untested! Furthermore, it is doubtful whether the test results of a hypothesis constructed out of a mathematical model with unreal assumptions could provide conclusive falsifying evidence to a theory unless the latter is extremely simple.

The mathematical economist might retreat to another route of defence. He could point out that even if qualitative variations of his concepts can hardly be fully ascertained, it would still be of importance that he builds formal models upon the polarities of his concepts. Such creations would shed light upon the broader structural aspects of the theory in question and would enable him to have an overall view of the theoretical limits of the theory that he formalizes. This way, he can still make important academic progress without being restricted by the problem of subsumption or qualitative variations. Such a defence, however, has to be qualified. Formalization that disregards qualitative variations and the study of polarities are two different affairs altogether. We may recall our discussion on acceptable or unacceptable distortion of reality in theoretical abstractions. Acceptable distortion amounts to a theory that what has been left out could be expected to be eventually explained by the implicit part of the theory, through additional or auxiliary assumptions. But qualitative distortion is the ignoring of the deeper complexities, rather than acknowledging the complexity but only studying a part of it. Study of polarities is, in this respect, similar to acceptable distortion in that it isolates the extreme or "pure" cases for study first while making the assumption that what has been left out could be explained later.

While the above criticisms should be pointing to the indefensibility of the formalization position, it is yet insufficient to supply a general explanation as to where and how such limitations of formalization spring from and thereby whether such limitations are avoidable or how they can be made up for. To answer this broader question, we have to examine the issue of formalization from both the growth-of-knowledge and the cognitive points of view.

NOTES
1. This has to presuppose of some kind of realism and perhaps the correspondence theory of truth.
2. But there are acceptable and unacceptable distortions as we have discussed in Chapter 1.

3.   The way in which qualitative variations are represented is through a differentiation of symbols. But even so, "quantification does not cause quality to vanish, it leaves a qualitative residual which perforce must be carried over into the numerical formula by which the phenomenon is described. Otherwise this formula would not constitute an adequate description. The problem is to find out under which form the qualitative residual is hidden in a purely numerical pattern" Géorgescu-Roegén, (1971, p.101).

4.   See, for instance, Jaynes (1976). Also see Fromm (1941).

5.   Following Isabelle Prigogine (1977).

6.   In his defence of the use of formalization in the realm of human sciences, Granger argues that science is able to overcome the ineradicable elements of subjective human interpretation of the social and psychological reality and that science can bring along its own systematic concepts and schemes of analysis onto the social and psychological reality. However Granger's arguments in his *Formal Thought and the Sciences of Man* (1983) amount to merely that we can impose a certain framework onto the social and psychological reality, as suits the present capacity and convenience of present theorizing techniques. His approach is unable to ask the question of what limitations are attached to such frameworks. His approach has, too, barred him from asking what crucial aspects of reality we want to penetrate into would be left out by such frameworks. His approach has made him fall prey to whatever first frameworks that look systematic and scientific to him and prevented him from asking whether the results of such "scientific" techniques are really relevant in the broader context of what we want to know.

7.   Cf. Walters' conclusion on production functions. "After surveying the problems of aggregation, one may easily doubt whether there is much point in employing such a concept as an aggregate production function. The variety of competitive and technological conditions we find in modern economies suggests that we cannot approximate the basic requirements of sensible aggregation except, perhaps, over firms in the same industry or for narrow sections of the economy" (1963, p.11).

8.   Ironically but not unexpectedly, quantification techniques are more suitable to the purposes of a command economy where individual variations are suppressed and ignored.

9.   For a more comprehensive argument, see Chapter 4 of this book.

Chapter Three
Epistemic Development of Social Science Theories[1]

Economists in the last few decades have been used to formalization as the chief vehicle for conducting research in economics. To arrest such a bias, it is not enough to merely point out the limited value of formalization. More importantly, we have to elucidate the potential harm of relentless application of formalization and the actual damage it has wrought upon the discipline. To do so, it is necessary to assess the overall methodological status of formalization from the broader perspective of epistemology, in particular from the perspective of the growth of scientific knowledge. For this task, we need to construct a growth-of-knowledge model for social sciences. We would first explicate the structural properties of the model and then appraise the role of formalization in its context.

This epistemic model for social sciences, though congenial in certain ways to the Kuhnian (1962) and Lakatosian (1970) models, provides a wider framework to develop theories about the logic of scientific discovery. It differs moreover from those models in essential aspects.[2] Built partly upon an *epistemic-situational foundation,*[3] this model also differs significantly from those developmental models espoused by Goffman (1971), Crane (1972), Radnitzky (1973), Mullins (1973), Mulkay (1975), etc. These other models invariably adopt the sociological or institutional perspective, even though some of the different stages constructed by these other models appear to resemble the epistemic model outlined in this chapter in so far as the demarcation lines are drawn from the methodological orientation.

The Embryonic or Coarse Structure

As a point of departure, let us postulate that we have an embryonic or coarse theoretical structure and we will start by tracing the development of this embryonic structure. Let us understand by an embryonic or coarse structure to be a set of *germinal* concepts and their postulated unifying principles which represent an initial stage of formulation of a theory or a group of related theories.[4] These germinal concepts and their underlying unifying principles would altogether constitute the *base system* or the *core structure* upon which secondary or other peripheral concepts and relations can be built. Should the coarse structure manage to grow, it might ultimately mature into an established domain[5] with a network of peripheral structures.

It is not necessary for our present purpose to go into detail how a particular embryonic structure comes into being.[6] Suffice it to presume that it generally emerges or arises against a background where a keen awareness develops among practitioners of a discipline or serious thinkers related to the discipline to look for an *alternative schema* to an existing domain. We might want, for instance, alternatives which open up realms of study that are broader than the discipline of the day and that are more in conformity with our intuitive notion of what should be the subject matter of that discipline. Lorenz's ethology, dedicated to the study of animal behavior and the units of action that constitute instincts, is a good example. Freud's notion of the unconscious[7] and Chomsky's notion of the deep structure of language are also paradigmatic examples of this kind. Or perhaps, we might want a new theoretical structure to handle a changing reality. Adam Smith's notions of division of labor and economic growth, for instance, were pro-

mpted by developments at the dawn of the Industrial Revolution
and at the same time were attempts to characterize aspects of such
developments. On the other hand, we might want alternatives which
can be stripped of metaphysically questionable assumptions. For example, Agassi (1964) has shown that an important and indispensable part of the history of development of physics was motivated
by metaphysical views, namely, action at a distance must be explained away and that pulling actions must be surface phenomena that
must ultimately be explained by push. Or one might even adopt the
Kuhnian model that the academic community feels that an alternative is needed that could better explain a growing number of
"anomalies" to the then received theories (Kuhn 1962).

It is a truism that not all competing coarse structures will finally
turn out to be the forthcoming received theory nor develop into an
alternative "paradigm" of the Kuhnian type. But it can be presumed that the more the established theories fail to conform with the
metaphysics of the day, the more these received theories are felt to
be too narrow in scope, and the more they fail to contain the
onslaught of new anomalies, the stronger is the need for more
coarse structures to be offered as competing alternatives. The promise to appear unproblematic to the prevailing metaphysics, to
widen the ambit of an existing discipline, or to accommodate known
anomalies — which are largely intuitively assessed potentials — thus
constitute favorable conditions for the admittance of a coarse structure as a budding alternative.[8]

The Unfolding of The Embryonic Structure

Upon admittance of a coarse structure as a promising alternative,
the growth of the coarse structure will follow several recognizable
steps, as a result of the necessarily incomplete and raw nature of any
initial idea. In the first instance, the coarse structure has to reconcile
itself with the domain of empirical knowledge i.e. all known, relevant facts and effects that lie within the purview of the existing domain, the supporting theoretical knowledge that constitute the

background to such a domain as well as other related or relevant knowledge systems.[9] In other words, it has to find for itself a proper place in the context of the old domain as well as the background knowledge[10] related to it. Alternatively, the new coarse structure has to provide a new context to accommodate or to reject the old domain. A kind of "interpretative-assimilative" process is thus set off, with all previously known facts and theories being interpreted systematically in light of the framework provided by the new coarse structure.

Hand in hand with such an interpretative-assimilative process is the process of materializing and extending the initially-hoped-for empirical potentials of the coarse structure, that is, its capacity in establishing new contacts with reality, in generating new empirical content or in colonizing domains of already well-worked-out theories. A kind of sprawl for access to reality and scramble for maximal reach to reality characterize this particular stage of development.

This may follow several steps. Concepts under the coarse structure which depict polarities in continuum of gradations in reality may be identified. Various qualitative variations or gradations that lie between these polarities may be discovered or identified as such. In turn concepts of these intermediate gradations become precisified and validated by checking with reality.[11] Relations between these gradations within polarities can then be discovered and in turn be precisified and validated against reality. After several rounds or steps, the qualitatively precisified coarse structure is being developed and substantiated into a full-fledged domain and being stretched to reach a wider territory of the human or social reality. From his notion of the unconscious, for instance, Freud was led to formulate his hypotheses of infantile sexuality and the Oedipus Complex, the theory of life and death instincts, of repetition compulsion, the theory of personality and character formation, together with a new theory of anxiety and so on.

Since maximal access to reality stands out as the dominant concern at this particular stage of development, the basic mode of enquiry is that of confirmation.[12] Propositions that are supported by confirming instances within the context of the coarse framework are admitted as provisionally sound, regardless of whether they will stand later tests. A kind of pragmatism thus prevails during this initial growing period of a coarse structure. It seems therefore that at the first stage of elaborating upon a potentially promising coarse structure, confirmation naturally and justifiably precedes other modes of enquiries. Such a position has however, to be qualified. In the embryonic stage of any theory, we can expect only certain broad basic features of the theory to be correct. It would be unreasonable to expect the full content of what is being proposed as being true of reality. Thus, a theory usually proceeds with only minimal testing just to make sure that it is not completely off the mark. This kind of minimal testing which knowingly does not satisfy full testing standards thus contributes to a bias towards confirmation, as well as the appearance of preoccupation with confirmation at this stage.

Correspondence with Reality

Subsequent to, or sometimes concurrent with, the unfolding of the coarse structure, the scramble for maximal access to reality gradually gives way to a different concern. As the pragmatist imperative of the earlier phase has gradually been completed, the question naturally arises whether or not the newly developed theories, which might sensitize us to an allegedly newly recognized part of reality, do really hold. Partly to correct the excesses of the earlier pragmatist imperative and partly to tighten the rules for admittance of new knowledge claims, a developing domain tends to reshuffle its priorities towards the criteria of whether or not and how far its knowlege claims, both new and old, correspond with reality. This concern thus gradually puts more stringent testing or full-fledged falsification as the major mode of criticism or appraisal criterion at this particular phase. Corollarilly, repairs or modifications made to the growing domain that result from testing become part and parcel of the priorities in this period. Thus, real and apparent (i.e. guarded and minimal testing) confirmation, falsification and modifications are essential activities related to different sub-phases of a coarse structure unfolding itself into a domain that put its chief concern first as that of reaching out far into the hitherto untrodden reality and then that of making sure that the theories being embraced are true of reality.[13] As a joint result of part or all of the above-mentioned activities, the unfolding coarse structure gradually takes shape of an established domain with a network of peripheral concepts as well as intermingled relations and theories.

The Parameter-Variable Dichotomy[14]

From what is depicted in the above sections, it would seem that with the gradual expansion of a coarse structure into a mature domain, the resultant structure would give a more precise and accurate description of reality, until all the potential of the coarse structure is exhausted. This is, however, usually not the case. In actuality, many social science theories deviate significantly in their development from this ideal pattern. Some of them do not have the capacity even at the stage of the coarse structure to grow into a domain that is anywhere near the reality. Some which have rich potentials in intuitive insights manage to grow up to a point, but then for some reasons, develop into rigid structures which gradually sever themselves from any links with reality. Others may have the capacity to grow but do not seem to be able to penetrate orderly or far into reality, or be grounded solidly on it. Many of them require, so to speak, "wholesale leaps of faith" to sustain their development, and even so, only manage to touch the fringes of reality. Common to these diverse and frequently delinquent developments is thus their inability to actualize the full potentials of a coarse structure on solid grounds. Almost invariably, such delinquent developments are attributable to both the initial endowment of insights and the accompanying methodological outlook of their practitioners.

To depict the different patterns of development, we could use the conventional variable versus parameter distinction and look into the different ways in which various theories or disciplines have handled the relations between their variables and parameters. We use the former to indicate within a coarse theoretical structure the set of elements or structural properties that are causally related directly to each other, independent variables indicating the causal factors, while the dependent variables elements that are causally acted upon by the causal factors. This set of variables thus forms a self-contained, "endogenous," or interior causal structure in itself and can be looked upon as the nucleus of a coarse structure, capable of being treated as a unit of analysis, or point of departure for analysis. Exogenous to this interior or core causal structure is a set of factors that indirectly but significantly shape the operation of the inner causal structure in question. We call these factors parameters. Such a dichotomy is useful because it enables theoretical analysis to be carried out in a step-wise manner. Systematic analysis can be carried out by examining first the causal structure itself and then its relation between each parameter separately or in combination. The parameters themselves may in turn be separately analyzed and their relations further spelled out. Such step-wise development is not only amenable to man's general thinking habits, but is also rooted in the fundamental fact that man has only limited attentional resources to spare at one time.

Such a dichotomy is especially relevant to the study of social science subjects. The manifested human reality as we experience invariably comes under a large number of intervening factors, some directly relevant, some indirectly so, some only remotely contributing to a particular situation, while still others too fuzzy to be clearly identified. Most of these factors, and their multifarious relations are too elusive to pin down and account for. To add to the problem, the human reality is characterized by its incessantly drifting towards new and unknown patterns as a result of dynamic interactions among its far-from-uniform agents, and the corresponding far-from-equilibrium human or social events. To handle such fuzziness in theoretical analysis, it is therefore necessary to first limit the scope of analysis to a few key endogenous variables and their basic causal structure while keeping out other factors as background parameters for the time being. Only until the basic causal structure is elucidated or given more precise formulation should we introduce further parameters. Given our humanly limitation to handle simultaneously an entire array of relevant factors and their multifarious relations, *orderly and controlled* analysis naturally represents the second-best solution. It is possible under such a schema of enquiry, at least in principle, to examine all known parameters in turn, to reshuffle the status of certain parameters and variables for more thorough-going analysis, to precisify the variables in question with each additional advancement of knowledge of the parameters as well as to introduce new parameters into an existing framework. In this way, the richness of reality can be captured in an orderly manner and the multifarious relations among human events can be systematically explored and cross-examined. Such an approach, too, can gradually extend the realm of an existing domain by interfacing it with related ones, resulting in leaps in its explanatory power.

The Fixation of Parameter-Variable Relations

Unfortunately, for one reason or another, such progressive steps are not always followed in the actual development of many social science theories. Quite the contrary, the development is, more often than not, directed towards the fixation of the interior causal structure or the parameter-variable relations, thus limiting the capacity for orderly and controlled analysis. Such fixation, or fossilization of the interior causal structure of a theory or its parameter-variable relations takes a variety of forms and several typical versions can be identified among well-known social science theories.

An extreme case of fossilization is represented by the behaviorist learning theory which accepts no other variables than its two core ones, i.e. stimulus and response. Corollarily, it refuses to see or to take into account parameters that may possibly relate to the basic stimulus-response schema, or that may pose conditions governing the various possible links between stimuli and responses. Such an extreme closure, needless to say, severs the theory from any meaningful contact with reality. Most studies of animal cognition focused on the gaining of an experimental control of learning processes in order to examine their nature. Stimulus-response theory leaves both consciousness and the "organism" out of account and is purely operational in its establishment of the laws under which animals learn. Even when, as in Hull's learning theory, the organism is introduced, its place is taken by a formal set of mediating processes in which neither mental life nor biological processes as such is revealed.[15] As a result, such a research programme has to rely upon infinite *ad hoc* adjustments of definitions and on their arbitrary mappings to experimental results in particular cases. Such an extreme closure is attributable to the behavorists' aspiration to their desire to create a "scientific" psychology in the most constricted sense, by purging whatever that does not seem to be "empirical" from their standpoint.

A slightly more relaxed form of fixation is that while the existence of parameters is acknowledged, they are tacitly stripped of any theoretical significance. They are either considered *ad hoc* conditions to particular cases or are just interpreted away as mere givens that the interior causal structure is autonomous of and thereby need not be taken into account. Marxism is a case in point. Endowed with strong interpretative power over reality, its internal framework is rendered so theoretically self-sufficient that no exogenous parameters are capable of penetrating into the framework, still less in modifying it towards realism.

Another form of fossilization grows around those theories or disciplines where their key endogenous variables are susceptible to "objective" measurement, analysis or testing, and thereby readily amenable to formal treatment. In these cases parameters external to the interior set of variables are admitted of their empirical relevance and hence their potential theoretical significance. Nonetheless, the interior set of endogenous variables is believed to be fundamental and as such, should remain unaltered as a point of departure, at least in their barest form. While it is agreed that progressive introduction of exogenous parameters is necessary in order to inject empirical content into the domain in question, it remains the firm practice of analysis to give first priority to precisify the endogenous variables and formalize their relations. It is believed that this primary task is essential to and can facilitate the later injection of content. Chomskian linguistics and mainstream economics fall into this particular mode of enquiry. On the surface, the argument for first formal precisification and then the orderly injection of content appears to stand. There are, however, insurmountable difficulties in execution and contrary to expectation, further development of the formalized set of endogenous variables and their relations usually drifts away from development towards realism. Instead, it tends to lean towards a mode of *self-sustaining formal reconstitution* which finally bars the possibilities of bringing in outside parameters back to the basic framework. We will come back to this development in more detail later in the chapter.

There remains, however, some social science theories whose routes of development are free of fossilization of their interior or core variables or their parameter-variable relations. Such theories are usually characterized by their possession of core variables which are not subject to quantification, nor in many instances, subject even to "objectivist" analysis. Many theories in psychology belong to this type. While such theories, being incapable of easy precisification, look inferior to other social science theories that develop through the formal route, they actually benefit on the whole and in the long run in their escape from the fossilization tendencies.[16] Consider Freudian psychology as an example. Subsequent theory developments after Freud took on a highly plastic mode, with substantial shift in emphasis in the original core variables and parameter-variable relations, leading thereby to rich post-Freudian developments. Jung, for instance, extended Freud's notion of the unconscious to his collective unconscious which contains the psychological heritage of humanity as a whole. The Neo-Freudian school, including Fromm, Kardiner, Sullivan, and Horney, inverted the core variables of Freud's structure, pushing social and cultural factors into the forefront as determinants of human behavior while subdueing biological factors into background parameters. Fromm, for instance, proposed that it is not sexual behaviour that determine character, but rather character that determines sexual behavior. While Freud took the Oedipus Complex as the source of all neurosis, Horney explained it in terms of basic anxiety. On the other hand, the Kleinian school enriched Freud's core notions through a deeper penetration into infantile experience, an hitherto unexplored region in the pre-Oedipal stage and through the introduction of a new variable, namely, the aggression instinct.

Such rich development is marred, at least in appearance, by the fact that some of these developments look less than "scientific." Jung's conception of the collective unconscious, for instance, is virtually not open to refutation. Horney never sufficiently clarified her basic concepts and she herself gave a very inadequate account of the actual details of psychic structure. We are told of the various neurotic traits but were given no understanding as to why that particular combination arose rather than any other. We are struck by the number of observations which her theory does not explain.[17] In some similar way, many of Fromm's ideas are even more "metaphysical" than Freud's. His bold conjecture about significant changes that have taken place in the human personality at certain historical epochs, though extremely interesting, remains largely speculative.

By comparison, the *"marginal-revisionist"* mode of theory development packaged in the formal language as found in economics or linguistics must appear much more orderly and hence more "scientific."[18] It is therefore not unnatural that at one stage and perhaps until now, mainstream economics with its elaborate logico-mathematical structures seemingly well-interfaced with reality through a host of descendant quasi-empirical models, is crowned the "Queen" of social sciences. As Debreu (1985) put it, "Among the social sciences, economics was in a privileged position to respond to that invitation (*i.e. the use of mathematics*),[19] for two of its central concepts, commodity and price, are quantified in a unique manner..... the prices in the economy are represented by a point in the price space, the real vector space dual of the commodity space. The rich mathematical structure of those two spaces provides an ideal basis for the development of a large part of economic theory.''[20] Like Freudian psychology, economics is initially blessed with rich germinal ideas passed on by its Classical economists. But unlike post-Freudian developments, these rich germinal ideas become gradually ossified into rigid parameter-variable relations subject first to formalization and then to a stage of *self-sustaining reconstitution process*. Much of this latter development, however, lies beyond the initial intention of the earlier economists who aim merely to quantify economic concepts for more precise analysis.

The Advent of Formal Reconstitution

Once the set of core variables of a theoretical structure becomes well-defined and quantitatively precisified while its related parameters are well pushed into the background, the formal structure isolated and erected becomes the basis for further analysis. In the study of production, the production function which formally relates output to different combinations of capital and labor, for instance, becomes the standard point of departure for subsequent formal analysis. Consider another example, the theory of economic growth. Adam Smith first outlined several crucial dimensions relevant to this phenomenon. He studied in considerable detail the productive power of labor, the role of the manufacturing sector and the importance of capital accumulation. Among these three main features, capital accumulation is the most readily quantifiable and formalizable. So in time, the structure of analysis grew around the formal analysis of capital accumulation while the other factors faded into the background. The former finally became the standard point of departure in the study of economic growth.

Once a standard point of departure becomes formalized and well accepted, the stage is set for further reconstitution of the domain through the proliferation of model-theoretic constructions taking the same point of departure. Instead of going back to study systematically those parameters that have been brushed aside "for the time being", as one would expect, subsequent development of theorization almost invariably drifts away from this important potential source of contact with reality. Instead, subsequent researches tend towards further analysis of the formal properties of the core variables, keeping essentially the same formal point of departure. There are compelling reasons for development towards this direction. First and foremost, it is technically difficult to introduce a non-formalizable or even less formalizable parameter into a well-formalized core structure. Indeed it may well be the case that the "scaffolding," as Kaldor (1972) called it, gets thicker and more impenetrable with every successive reformulation of the theory, with growing uncertainty as to whether there is a solid building underneath. Second, formal reconstitution always gives the impression of making progress in knowledge. This impression is founded upon the fact that formal reconstitution often renders existing knowledge more transparent and easier to comprehend. It also enables important hidden relations to stand out and redundant assumptions to be discriminated. This is particularly the case where the amount of content in a domain has accumulated to the point where it becomes desirable, if not altogether necessary, to reorganize it for more efficient processing, or for more effective comprehension by the "mind."[21] Furthermore, reconstitution facilitates the elimination and the reconciliation of inconsistencies. In other words, the reconstitution of a mature domain for cognitive efficiency and effectiveness is somehow a logical development.[22] Finally, formal reconstitution enables us to enquire into the ultimate boundary or the theoretical limits of a domain that begins to take shape, thereby throwing light on the overall development potentials of a maturing domain.

Formal reconstitution, however, triggers several important consequences. Reconstitution invariably requires or implies a temporary fixation of the basic relations between the original concept and the source experience from which such concepts were derived or by which the creation of these concepts was prompted. This fixation is usually meant to be provisional, and is often well qualified. As a result the initial fixation itself is not harmful as long as the purpose of the fixation is still being remembered and understood. What is harmful is that over time, the original context is forgotten and the fixation becomes taken for granted. That is, the fuller intuitive appreciation of reality that prompts the development of the coarse structure in the first place becomes lost. What other aspects of reality that the reconstituted concepts have left out and for what reasons, have been lost sight of. Thus, the ability or at least the mental agility to develop alternative concepts to capture the same part of reality is incapacitated.

It follows then that what is originally being presumed is no longer questioned. Accordingly, the theoretical constructs that grow out of such presumptions gradually acquire the image of having a more solid foundation that they actually have. What are initially tolerable first fixations become "solid" grounds for further buildup, and as reconstitution activities intensify, more and more fixations become necessary in a mature domain. Not only does it become necessary to freeze the original concepts and its presumed relations, it gradually becomes necessary to freeze the first-order theoretical constructs, *ad infinitum*. A kind of "wholesale" freezing in a hierarchical manner emerges as the processes go on indefinitely. Habitual assumption thus creates its own false authority.

To facilitate formalization and for modelling consistency, it is often necessary to alter an orginal concept, or to reject a more pregnant version. For example, Menger's original exposition of marginal utility in terms of a hierarchy of wants, being incompatible with calculus, the formal technique of the day, was dropped in spite of its richer and more true-to-life content.[23] Even modern-day economists prefer to stay with the axioms of conventional formal consumer theory because it is exceedingly difficult to formalize ideas such as lexicographic preference systems. In many cases, the original concept has to be "extremitized" or "idealized." Thus we have the notion of the economic man with its peculiar behavioral assumptions which run counter to our common sense. For consistency, his choices must be transitive, a point which is not universally borne out by facts. For completeness, he must be able to rank all his preferences in respect of different combinations in a bundle of goods, an absurd, if not impossible task for an ordinary man. In a somewhat similar manner, the notion of indifference, introduced to replace the elusive notion of utility, bears little analogue with real life situations. Consumers do not always face indifference situations while some of the indifference situations he actually faces merely signify his failure to make up his mind rather than his rational calibration of his preferences. In other words, reconstitutions tend to create a new family of concepts into a domain, which either replace existing concepts, or where the originals are not easily replacable, modify them to generate a new set of notions or ideas. This possibility is well put by Debreu (1985), "The divorce of form and content immediately yields a new theory whenever a novel interpretation of a primitive concept is discovered. A textbook illustration of this application of the axiomatic method occurred in the economic theory of uncertainty. The traditional characteristics of a commodity were its physical description, its date, and its location when in 1953 Kenneth Arrow proposed adding the state of the world in which it will be available. The reinterpretation of the concept of a commodity led to a theory of uncertainty which eventually gained broad acceptance, notably among finance theorists."

But what are generated as "new" concepts or theories through this route are not new in the sense we would usually expect. They are not new with respect to knowledge about the external reality. What is "new" is essentially implicit in the mode of analysis being undertaken. For example, we would expect the generation of the molecular clock theory of species evolution, given the state of molecular biology and anthropology as well as with the mathematics they employ. Thus what is new is the logical product of the method of analysis. The newness is relative to the mathematics used and to the inner structure of the theory, in particular to the theoretical limits of a domain.

In physical sciences, reconstitutions serve important purposes. They help to locate or discover new unifying relations between different sub-domains or to yield the most powerful representation of what content that has been captured. As can be expected, some major advances in the understanding of physics are associated with formal reconstitutions. The theory of electromagnetism which unifies electricity and magnetism into a single theory by Maxwell, the integration of electromagnetic and weak nuclear forces into a unified theory by Weinberg and Salam are the results of recasting existing domains in new mathematical descriptions. But the situation with economic theories is very different. Here many important notions are not directly measurable, and those that depend on aggregation for their meaning have very dubious status. Much reconstitution within economic theories centering around only those variables that are directly measurable or their dubious aggregates is of a qualitatively different nature compared with reconstitution in physics.

Once set off, these formal reconstitutive processes start interacting with and reinforcing one another. New theoretical constructs enable existing knowledge to be reinterpreted and the reconstitution of existing theories may require new theoretical constructs to act as intermediaries. This in turn may lead to the emergence of new theoretical constructs. Likewise, reinterpretation of existing empirical content in light of new theoretical constructs or newly reconstituted theories may lead to further unifying relations or concepts. In this way, the whole domain is part by part and probably more than once being rebuilt.

Extra-Empirical Orientation

Reconstitution and its products demand an entirely different set of appraisal criteria. The criterion of correspondence with reality, even if it still remains important, will gradually fade into the background as "extra-empirical" or "super-empirical" criteria are being applied and expanded. For to appraise reconstituted concepts and theories, we need extra-empirical criteria such as rigor, requirements of symmetry, simplicity, conformity with certain *a priori* conditions, metaphysical postulates, etc.[24] These new criteria of appraisal both constitute and provide the heuristics to guide the development of further reconstitutions.

As already pointed out, these processes feed on themselves. In principle, it is possible to reconstruct without limit theoretical constructs, and to reconstitute theories upon theories. An original concept, upon fixation and closure, is the object of study and reconstruction. In turn, the reconstructed concept becomes the object of study and further reconstruction. The consequence of this "extra-empirical" orientation is that in time, the domain will expand not so much through the widening of its empirical base, which is limited any way, as through the proliferation of layers of reconstructed concepts and reconstituted theories, as well as the vast amount of corresponding appraisal work and its aftermaths which, too, are limitless activities. Such proliferation is attributed further to the fact that the basic notions embodied in some of the appraisal criteria are rather ambiguous. For example, there can be different and sometimes partially conflicting explications of the notion of simplicity. In the absence of unambiguous notions or ways of defining the optimal relations between these different criteria, it is possible to reconstruct multiple and even competing accounts of a given domain. In a similar way, it is always possible to investigate without limit the properties of the theoretical limits of models constructed upon postulating different permutations of theoretical limits of the first order and so on. With such a wide array of reconstitutional dimensions and possibilities, the shift of research emphasis from empirical work towards the extra-empirical or "structural"[25] aspects of the domain becomes a logical development. There is thus an "epistemic inevitability" in the shift of attention from empirical content to extra-empirical structure as a domain undergoes intense reconstitutions.

The Consequences of Self-Sustaining Formal Reconstitution

As the concern over extra-empirical structures takes over, the now established or articulated domain will undergo changes which will finally bring about its decline. One consequence of this extra-empirical orientation is that empirical content has to be traded off.[26] First, certain types of extra-empirical studies, like axiomatization or the construction of prototypes, require that the less relevant empirical contents be trimmed. Second, as the extra-empirical concerns start to dominate, the empirical content of the domain undergoes changes too. In part, this is the result of the incessant reinterpretative activities which turn the original set of empirical content into expanded multiples of reinterpreted content. In time, such expanded content resulting after a number of reinterpretations becomes fused with and embodies within it more and more theoretical constructs of different orders. As a consequence it becomes increasingly *"domain-specific,"* i.e. it can be fully understood only through the translation of specific vocabulary, or the decoding of definitions and correspondence rules. Ample examples of this type can be found in both modern linguistics and mainstream economics. Up to a point, whatever empirical content that a domain is currently possessing or interested in gathering is bound to be heavily *"structure-laden"* or *"domain-laden."* It is bound to be indirect in that it may have to be decoded probably a number of times before it can be mapped back to the propositions that talk about the real world. Conversely, new research products within the domain, be they the reconstitution of theories or the building of peripheral structures, would have by proportion less empirical content as the amount of extra-empirical knowledge in the domain accumulates.

As the domain-specific content of a domain as opposed to its empirical content grows, the domain in turn undergoes a kind of internalization process, with more and more research resources being directed towards the buildup and elucidation of its internal structures, or analogous to what Kuhn puts it, towards "puzzle-solving activities" (Kuhn, 1962). In economics and linguistics, this leads to the development of a wholesale formalism, as the knowledge within its various domains is almost completely rewritten in terms of formal concepts and operations. In parallel, new efforts expended within these domains concentrate more and more on trivial issues, although this is not the sole result of extra-empirical activities. Even without the latter, such development is unavoidable as the empirical potential of a domain is gradually heading towards exhaustion.

Wholesale formalization is by no means a neutral activity from the epistemic viewpoint, for it implies a reordering of the knowledge captured within a domain in line with the syntactical properties of the mathematics employed, which may not necessarily reflect its empirical significance. That part of knowledge that is more amenable to formal and mathematical treatment would naturally be singled out while the rest be kept in the background. A kind of "organized distortion" of the domain gradually takes place as wholesale formalism develops and as reconstitution continues.

With this *"intra-domain reshuffle"* of knowledge tilting towards extra-empirical considerations, the concern for correspondence fades. The major appraisal criterion that comes to foreground is that of coherence. Whether the content stands the test of reality is no longer of foremost importance. At the same time, as the domain is overloaded with extra-empirical knowledge, it becomes more difficult to test the empirical content in question. There are two aspects to this latter phenomenon. First, academicians are more inclined to preserve a well-developed logical edifice even at the risk of failure to match or further capture reality. Psychological and institutional factors apart, it seems less risky to lean on a framework that has proven its merit or that has been well corroborated, particularly in the absence of viable competing frameworks. *Ad hoc* auxiliary assumptions and immunizing stratagem (Popper, 1972) are likely to develop in order to protect the hard core (Lakatos, 1970) from being falsified. Furthermore, with the accumulation of extra-empirical knowledge, it would be more difficult to falsify the more important propositions of the domain, even if no conscious protection work is done. New empirical data that may be available to test a proposition will naturally face increasing difficulty penetrating into the hard core which is now shielded by levels of reinterpreted content and proliferated peripheral structures.[27] In addition, the empirical data available for falsification may themselves have to be interpreted or reinterpreted before they can function as useful falsifiers in the now hierarchically ranked domain. As a result, efforts directed to falsification are bound to be futile at this particular phase. With the threat of falsification virtually removed, the domain is liable to become more *error-insensitive*. This, together with the trend towards trivialization, will sap the now "extra-empirical-structure-laden" domain of its further capacity to talk about and to correspond with the real world.

Law of Diminishing Yield of Empirical Content

At one stage or another, an established and expanding domain that grows either through the route of formal reconstitution or the restructuring of its parameter-variable relations towards more realism will face exhaustion of potential of its original concepts. One finds that older theories become more and more unclear when one tries to use them to obtain insight into new domains (Bohm 1980). In the case of formal reconstitution, recognition of this problem may be indefinitely delayed, although it would be clear that the more a domain undergoes reconstitution, the more it would be cut off from reality. In whichever case, a maturing domain will develop towards the limit of its capacity to capture reality, be it a natural or an artificially imposed one. Such natural limit exists because any theoretical structure is, by its very nature, selective in what it seeks to unify. Conversely, it naturally excludes or keeps untouched certain aspects of reality without necessary knowledge of their "ultimate" relevance. The basic operative principles of the market economy as we know of, for instance, cannot be extended without drastic alterations to explain the undeveloped or primitive economies. There is, therefore, "an essential incompleteness" of any man-made theoretical system and indeed of any science (Popper 1982).[28]

There is another compelling reason why a coarse structure must in time be exhausted of its capacity to be elaborated and refined upon to reflect reality. This is because all theoretical structures are in principle "level-bound." Theoretical systems of different levels or orders cannot be entirely reduced, not even in principle, to one base system. Even in the realm of the natural sciences, "philosophical reductionism" does not hold. New axioms have to be added at each new level in order to derive significant propositions about the theoretical system of the new level (Popper 1982). In other words, we may grant for the sake of argument that we have presently at hand a fully developed structure which has captured perfectly some aspects or parts of reality. Our desire for deeper understanding into reality, for further knowledge of the ramifications of that part of reality we already understand, and our quest for knowing how one part of reality is related to another, will surely in time tax that structure beyond its potentials.

In the social sciences, the impossibility of complete reduction is further reinforced by the fact that its atomic units, i.e. the individual human beings that constitute the social reality, are aware of each other's reactions. Such awareness is constantly in a state of change, systematic or random, sensible or stupid. People carry around with them conceptions — right or wrong — about what their social environment is like and how that environment would behave. They react differently according to their different conceptions about how other people behave and how their social environment would behave. While it is useful for instance, to have a theory of personality in order to understand the individual in society, the theory in question would be grossly inadequate to explain group behavior and the emotional dynamics of the group. At which point collective behavior remains a summation of individual reactions and at which point collective behavior begins to represent a departure from such a summation will remain an open question. This renders it impossible to tell precisely at what particular point collective actions will trigger qualitative changes in the overall result.[29]

Carrying this "finite-capacity thesis" further, it appears that a kind of "law of diminishing yield of empirical content" characterizes the development of a coarse structure into an established domain, as the growth area turns from the core to the periphery. New empirical contents added are likely to become localized, less significant and less interesting. This applies equally well to those theories whose growth relies on formal reconstitution. However, for the latter theories we can expect spurts of growth of empirical knowledge at the point they manage to shed the chains of formalism.

The Emergence of A New Cycle

While the decline of any theoretical domain is by and large predictable and is thus a matter of time, it is, however, difficult to tell what will follow next. It is possible for a declining domain to drag on for a considerable period, depending on the institutional inertia or the prevailing academic ethos. Such institutional factors may facilitate or hinder the development of new coarse structures and the willingness to invest effort into elaborating, justifying and testing them. Where radical change is to take place, it is not possible to tell beforehand the nature of the change. Broadly speaking, there are several common courses of development. On the one hand, fresh concepts may be injected into the existing domain, thereby providing it with a chance to expand its empirical boundary. The resulting domain may appear less objectionable according to the prevailing conceptions of the nature of reality (i.e. metaphysics). Or it may give more hope about throwing light on those areas which our intuitive notion of the subject regards as the proper subject matter of that discipline, but which the previous theory has not be able to explain. Or, in a Kuhnian vein, the resulting domain will be more able to explain anomalies that have been accumulated but so far left unexplained and unassimilated. Whether the rejuvenation represents a full recovery or merely a temporary relief cannot, again, be known *a priori*. Alternatively, the existing domain may be linked to other related domains, thus expanding its boundary through its fusion with them. The linkage may, of course, take a variety of forms. It may simply be absorbed into a broader domain and be reduced to being a special or limiting case of that broader structure. Or it may join with other domains of similar levels to form themselves into a large one. Or perhaps the whole domain simply fades into the background as new competing coarse structures are conceived, inculcated and finally become accepted. [30]

Whether fresh content would be injected into a mature domain, or whether a domain would be merged with or absorbed into another, or whether it would simply fade away, internal conflict would characterize the later stage of a mature domain. Conflicts will take place between revisionists who are prepared to trim only part of the established domain and radicals who want to abandon the entire framework and replace it by new ones. In other words, a new orthodoxy does not spring up full-blown. Instead it will be instated in its entrenched position through a long process of intellectual competition, a position taken by the later Kuhn (1970).

It is, however, difficult to chart precisely the pattern of development beyond this point. At each stage of development into the next, possibilities of developing through alternative routes always exist. Which of these possibilities will be materialized or be missed out would be governed in part by historical factors particular to the history of a subject and the overall intellectual background of that age. Thus to predict the development of any single discipline in greater detail and precision, we would need to study the logic of the intellectual situation of academicians individually and as a whole, how they view their then existing domain, how far they are prepared to abandon or revise it, and how they balance the costs and benefits of radical or moderate changes. We would have to project how difficulties of one kind or another that new coarse structures will face as well as how far they will pose threats to the existing domain. This interesting study lies, however, beyond the scope of the present work.

Should the course of change take place in the form of a new coarse structure being accepted as a competing alternative to the existing domain, the same patterns of development that we have described in the foregoing paragraphs would likely repeat, until or unless we would develop new sets of methodologies that break such patterns. Regardless of the patterns that might actually be materialized, we seem to be in a position to surmise that on the whole, a kind of "epistemic cycle" characterizes the growth and development of knowledge in the social sciences, and to some extent in the natural sciences as well.[31] With the passage of each cycle, we can reasonably expect some improvement in our knowledge of the real world, although this is very different from saying that we can expect to acquire finally true knowledge about the world or knowledge that is incapable of being further improved. [32] Each cycle may bring us nearer to the truth, but there is no warrant whatsoever to support the bolder view that we will finally be there if we work long and hard enough.

The epistemic development depicted in the above is a meta-theory about the development of social science theories in general and should therefore be looked upon, short of new intervening factors that may emerge, as a broad epistemic sketch of how social science theories are born, how they grow, mature, decline and finally get replaced, or as elegantly put by William James, "the classic stages of a theory's career."[33] This meta-theory is not restricted to theories of a particular scale and it is perhaps as applicable to a small theoretical structure as to a whole discipline, although much additional knowledge would be needed in elucidating the development of the latter. No particular theory will perhaps follow precisely the same steps outlined in the above. The significance of this epistemic sketch lies rather in its capacity to highlight some important epistemic features or universals (Pandit, 1983) that characterize different types of social science theories. These epistemic features, including the fossilization of parameter-variable relations, the finite capacity to capture reality by a coarse structure, the shift of attention from empirical content to extra-empirical concern, the degeneration of the extra-empirical-structure-laden domain etc., provide some kind of situational logic that helps us to chart broadly the course of development of man's theoretical outputs. [34] It may be interesting to point out that part of these epistemic universals can perhaps be causally related to man's cognitive universals, although this is not the proper place to pursue this point further.[35]

NOTES

1. I am indebted to Bruce Caldwell for his critical comments on this chapter. Part of the rewriting of my manuscript is prompted by his criticism.
2. See footnote 33 below.
3. "Epistemic-situational" is coined here to indicate a departure from the received approach to philosophy of science which can be interpreted as epistemic-structural. Within this interpretation, the Popperian framework is by and large epistemic-structural. His growth of knowledge perspective and his conception of the logic of the situation etc. can be said to foreshadow the epistemic-situational approach espoused here. The Lakatosian framework can also be classified as essentially epistemic-structural, while Kuhn's framework could be better described as epistemic-sociological.
4. Compare Conant's theme that "science is an interconnected series of concepts and conceptual schemes" (1951, p.25).

5. The usage here bears some but not full resemblance to Shapere's concept of "scientific domain."

6. At the extreme, this is related to the controversial issue of whether there is a "logic of discovery." The question is unfortunately often confused by different meanings of the word "logic" being used.

7. The notion of the unconscious was, however, not originated by Freud.

8. Work on the growth of scientific knowledge indicates that the acceptance or rejection of general hypothesis as true plays a relatively minor role in the rational evaluation of hypothesis — science being concerned for the most part with evaluating, for example, whether an hypothesis is sufficiently promising to warrant further investigation, development and so on. See Fredrick Suppe (1977, p.631).

9. All these represent conditions imposed on the growing coarse structure by other theories or by extra-theoretic "framework principles" as Thomas Nickles called it (Suppe, 1977, p.573). They provide both the constraints as well as the heuristics to a growing coarse structure.

10. For the present purpose, it is not essential to distinguish different types of background knowledge, say, after Musgrave.

11. No severe test is to be expected.

12. The role of confirmation is of special importance in the social sciences. The fundamental problem in social sciences, at least at this very stage of development, appears to be that of extracting the right variables from the complexities of human phenomena. In other words, the fundamental task that confronts the social scientist is the question of discovery, as well as its most immediate corollary, namely, the question of confirmation. Premature emphasis on the question of falsification with its likely consequence of eliminating budding ideas is therefore liable to be counterproductive. This does not, however, mean that the abstractions made at this stage need not be rationally criticized. What ought to be done rather is the development of some different but more appropriate modes of criticism or appraisal criteria for use during this initial phase of the epistemic cycle, although such modes of criticism etc. are expectedly likely to be relatively lenient.

13. For the purpose here, it is not necessary to take side on the issue of confirmation versus falsification, nor to favor any particular theory of evidential support. Suffice it here to distinguish the respective roles of confirmation and falsification in different phases of an epistemic cycle.

14. I am indebted to Peter T. Bauer whose comments on my other book inspired me with the significance of employing such a dichotomy in the

analysis of social science theories. William Frazer's comments on my manuscript also helped me towards this development. This scheme of analysis here goes beyond the conventional critique of the *ceteris paribus* method.

15. See Crook (1980, p.6).

16. Somewhat expected, mathematical psychology has a small role to play in the development of the discipline. What areas that are formalized are very restricted and the formalized products are seldom exciting.

17. See Brown (1961) for a brief introduction.

18. Strictly speaking, theories that remain free of fossilization influences must be considered superior to those that become fossilized and subsequently formalized. The former though speculative in nature still remains in good contact with reality while the latter gradually severs its links with reality.

19. Added by the author.

20. Debreu made this statement in a different context.

21. "Without some such coherence conditions, it is clear that a world described by even a small number of predicates in all possible combinations is likely to become quickly unmanageable." See Mary Hesse (1980, p.126).

22. This is somewhat congenial to Shapere's conception of the "domain problems."

23. I owe this point to Peter Earl.

24. Cf. Mary Hesse's "coherence conditions" (1980, p.vii).

25. This is different from the study of the structural aspects of the content of a theory, by which we refer to the properties of uniformity, reproducibility, repetitiveness, standardization, typicality etc. of the variables of a domain.

26. It should, however, not be ruled out that certain studies of the extra-empirical structure of a domain may accidentally open up new areas for empirical enquiries.

27. Compare Lakatos's concept of the "protective belt" of auxiliary hypothesis, but which contains the flexible parts of a scientific research programme. See Lakatos (1970, pp.91-138).

28. This does not entail, however, that the ultimately developed and mature domain cannot explain new events or hitherto unforeseen relations in reality.

29. The magnitude of aggregation that triggers a qualitative change may represent merely a surface phenomenon and could possibly be accounted for in qualitative terms. This, however, does not invalidate the statement made here.

30. There can be a variety of routes whereby a new coarse structure is first conceived. Recent findings in cognitive science seem to support the thesis that some sort of "analogical reasoning" often plays a central role. "There is no lack of examples in the history of science where the structure of theories in a new subject area has been borrowed from, or at least suggested by, theories *in situ* in some quite different domain: what's known about the structure of the solar system gets borrowed to model the structure of the atom..." See Fodor (1983, p.107).

31. In a subject like rational mechanics, the only remaining problems are formal ones, and there is room for mathematical refinements alone: in more typical sciences, there is room for conceptual changes also, and this is what keeps them "scientific." Far from a typical science forming a complete logical system, it is its logical gaps and inconsistencies that keep the subject alive as an active developing field for scientific inquiry; and its very typical, unsystematic, nonaxiomatic character is what generates the real head of steam behind its problems (Toulmin, 1977, p.611).

32. This does not mean that each and every new coarse structure advanced need to promise progress in knowledge. But it should be sufficiently safe to say that one fully articulated domain that transcends and encompasses a previous one does represent an improvement in our knowledge. Since each addition of "passable" knowledge gradually becomes assimilated into our intellectual and academic tradition, such additions become in turn a tool or a step for our acquisition of further knowledge. Progress in knowledge can thus be viewed from two dimensions, namely it can be progressive in relation to past knowledge and can also be progressive in relation to the improvability of man's cognitive inputs in a broad sense. In other words, the present author is committed to a minimal position of both metaphysical and epistemological realism.

33. The conception of the epistemic cycle as espoused here, while bearing superficial resemblances to Kuhn's conception of "paradigm" and Lakatos's conception of the "research programme", must be viewed as substantially different from them in essential aspects. Stemming from the epistemic-situational approach as opposed to the epistemic-sociological (Kuhn) or the epistemic-structural approach (Lakatos), it provides a wider context to the logic of scientific discovery and development. It differs radically from Kuhn's paradigm in that: (a) it rejects the notion of incommensurability and its implications for relativism; (b) different coarse structures, growing domains and established domains can always co-exist; (c) the epistemic cycle is not restricted to theories of any scale; only at the

extreme of embracing the whole discipline need it be identified with the concept of the paradigm. It differs from Lakatos's position in that: (a) it is by and large not a prescriptive approach; (b) the locus of scientific progress can be an isolated theory or a series of theories; (c) it provides a stage-of-development analysis in a situational context, whereby Lakatos's concepts of positive and negative heuristics, of progressive and degenerative research programs, of mature and immature science etc. fall neatly into place. The notion of the epistemic cycle espoused here in fact comes a little nearer Shapere's conception of "field", where postulates of rationality, generalizability and systematizability are taken into account. It differs here, however, from Shapere's position in that it presents a broader account of the logic of scientific discovery and development by incorporating developments in social science theories. Though also congenial to Toulmin's concept of "scientific discipline" embedded in his evolutionary model of conceptual change and intellectual ecology, which encompasses not only internal and external history, but also the sociology of science, the psychology of scientific research and philosophy of science, the epistemic-cycle theory here is nevertheless essentially "epistemic."

34. It would be interesting to correlate each major stage of epistemic development with the various theories of truth in philosophy. Three general and competing types of theories of truth can be identified, namely the correspondence theories, coherence theories and pragmatic theories. The epistemic-cycle perspective espoused in this paper appears to be able to accommodate all these three theories within one roof by ascribing a proper role to each of the insights captured by the respective theories. Thus the first phase of the cycle where the fundamental concerns of a coarse structure, i.e. those of explaining existing anomalies and maximizing access to reality are essentially pragmatic, can be broadly identified with the pragmatic theories of truth. Similarly, the third stage of the epistemic cycle where attention is moved towards the extra-empirical aspects of the well-articulated domain can be associated with the coherence theories. It is not unreasonable to conjecture, therefore, that these three apparently competing theories of truth, each valid within a particular phase of the epistemic cycle and each representing merely a different epistemic appraisal criterion, are actually compatible and complementary with one another within this broader context.

35. For this thesis of cognitivism, see, for instance, Weimer (1974, p.376).

Chapter Four
Theory Metamorphosis and
the Role of Epistemic Archetypes

Unlike formal enquiries in logic and mathematics which are free to explore all sorts of logical possibilities and which thus face few constraints in their building of logical edifices, formalization in economics is constrained by the consideration that it is not the ultimate end in itself and that it has to take into account the question of whether the formal model corresponds with reality even in the most indirect manner. Inescapably, the significance of formalization has to be subjected and subordinated to the more important goal of congruence with reality.

With this added constraint in the background, we now proceed to the appraisal of the significance of formalization in economics, taking into account the theory of epistemic development cycle that we have developed in the last chapter. First we wish to demonstrate the limited significance of the formal method in economic enquiries, and indeed in enquiries in social sciences as a whole,[1] significance here indicates the potential in generating content for a theoretical domain. We will then examine in more detail the potential damage that formalization might inflict on the development of an economic or social science theory.

The Relative Impotence of Formalization in Social Sciences

We have shown that the potential content of a theory is by and large being captured or governed by its coarse structure, i.e., the structure in the formative phase. Most work that follows in the growing domain is related to the "unfolding" of the potential of the initial coarse frameworkexcept in the case where the fossilization of its parameter-variable relations and its subsequent drift towards formal reconstitution bar the fulfilment of such potentials. As a crude analogy, we can liken the initial coarse structure to the genes of all lives, the material which acts as a blueprint or program to direct the sequence of chemical processes that make up the life cycle of each cell. The most crucial step in social science theorizing thus consists of discovering the right coarse structure. The remaining activities that follow, whether they be the discovery of qualitative variations, the qualitative precisification of sub-concepts signifying such variations or the formalization of the essential concepts, rely very much on the quality and potential of this coarse structure and play only a supplementary, albeit indispensable role in the subsequent course of development.

In the physical sciences, in particular in the case of physics, formalization plays the dual role of spelling out systematically the content of a domain and of eliminating redundancies and inconsistencies. In this way, formalization is crucial to the growth of knowledge. Formalization in the social sciences, however, has a much restricted role. The restriction as previously pointed out is caused by the difference in the causal structure of the social reality. Formalization is effective in physics because nature can be taken as workably uniform, i.e., uniform over a presumably broad range of values of the variables in the formulae employed, and because it is possible for us to concentrate without much distortion on those parts of the physical reality that are most amenable to mathematical concepts[2] (Ziman, 1978, pp. 28-29). In social sciences, these are hardly the cases. Concepts in social sciences are liable to subsume significant qualitative variations that defy ready formalization, a point which we have dealt with in depth in a preceding chapter.

We have also shown that as a coarse structure has more or less exhausted its developmental possibilities, one most fruitful way out of the exhausted domain is to discover a new coarse structure which has the potential to capture new content, one which may render the existing domain a special case or one which may assimilate all known anomalies hitherto unexplained. The formal method which can operate effectively only upon given material is therefore not a useful tool for creative enquiries of this kind. The formal method can hardly be useful for, if not obstructive of, the pursuit of new coarse structures in social sciences.

The Limited Role of Formalization in Falsification in Social Sciences

In the case of the physical sciences, formalization plays an indispensable role in testing and falsification.[3] This role, however, is of much less significance in the case of the social sciences. There are two reasons for this. First, falsification in social sciences can be appropriately conducted in a qualitative mode. To test a particular social science theory, we could examine and test the implications of the theory in broad terms, namely, what kind of event-patterns would arise if the theory holds, what kind of event-patterns would be absent if the theory is valid, and what kind of event-patterns would contradict the theory. This approach is essentially qualitative, since the determination of the presence or absence of certain event-patterns does not of necessity require the quantification of relations between the variables in a particular theory.

Indeed, such a qualitative mode of testing and falsification is more appropriate and relevant to a large part or to certain important phases in the development of social sciences theories. Theories in social sciences do not and cannot predict individual occurrences in the order of our daily life.[3] They are about the deep structural mechanisms which constitute the broad framework within which individual occurrences materialize. Thus prediction in social sciences has to be prediction in principle, and not prediction of particular events (Hayek, 1967). This is because there is always an element of indeterminancy of behavior at the micro-level of the individual. This unpredictability is attributable to the fact that considerable individual differences exist as to how the individual adapts to new situations, how he learns from past experiences, and how he reacts to the fact that he is an object under study in certain testing situations. Such individual differences are inescapable for the reason that each individual possesses a unique though convergent background of knowledge, and that each has a different though by and large congenial repertoire of language habits and thinking tools.

Falsification in social sciences being essentially a qualitative instrument, the formal method can have only a limited contribution in this regard. Falsification via the formal method is able to help, but only to a limited extent, the correction and revision of a theory. Discrepancies between the model and the reality can be pointing to the existence of qualitative variations hitherto undiscovered, or can reveal changes of certain aspects in reality so far presumed to be invariants, or can indicate wrongly postulated relations between the concepts in question. However, as a formal model is continually being revised to take into account finer qualitative variations, that it, when it should then be in a better and better position to correspond to reality, the resulting formal models that remain to be constructed are likely to be more localized, to have lesser content, and conversely to have a smaller field of applicability. Thus it is likely that each falsification of a formal model may lead to the construction of new models of lesser content instead of a global model that can assimilate all anomalies. Consequently and paradoxically, the more a formal model is true of reality, the more trivial it is likely to be.

Such a pattern of development rests on the consideration that there is no *a priori* reason why there must exist certain formal techniques that can represent precisely within one global formal model new qualitative variations that have been or yet to be discovered. Quite the contrary, it appears more realistic to presume that with the discovery of finer qualitative variations, separate formal models have to be developed to reflect these variations on an individual or *ad hoc* basis. This plausibility is grounded on the reason that each qualitative variation subsumed under a common concept is likely to be generated by a set of causal factors or mechanisms that may have no or few relations to those factors and mechanisms underlying other variations. There is, for instance, no reason to presume that the principles governing manual skills can be equally applicable to managerial skills and that both can be covered neatly by the same formal techniques initially developed to handle the concept of labor as a whole. Similarly, it would be naive to lump together for the same formal treatment investments that are small, short-term and for established markets which therefore depends largely on ready market data, with investments on long-range, gigantic and essentially innovative projects, decisions of which depend essentially on *rationalistic parameters,* such as projections of income *per capita,* demographic trends, market shares, etc.

Even Granger (1983, pp.136-37), in his most enthusiastic support of the application of the formal method to human sciences, has not lost sight of such limitation. "Surrendering any pretension to a largely synthetic organization of the object, the axiomatic enterprise becomes essentially a means of local research which can only constitute its object piecemeal. While the epistemological space of the natural sciences approach the Euclidean type, that of the sciences of man seems to be in essence Riemannian. For the former, we can draw extended maps which immediately reveal its global structures. For the latter, only local explorations appear to be effective, leaving open the problem of relating two schemes of 'neighboring' regions. It would be quite imprudent to decide whether or not it will be possible to formulate a connecting law which would one day unify our knowledge. All that can be said is that today our knowledge progresses only in this groping way, which is perhaps essential for it." In the same vein, another conclusion we may draw from the above is that by the time a formalized theory is so revised that it is supposed to be capable of truly reflecting reality and free of further qualitative variations being subsumed, it will then have little content left. What reality it is then capable of reflecting is likely to have very limited significance, if not entirely uninteresting.

The preceding paragraphs should thus show the limited relevance of the formal method to the potential of generating or even enriching the content of a particular domain. This conclusion should not be surprising, for as we have shown in the exposition of the epistemic development of a social science theory, the key role of formalization lies in its capacity to elucidate certain structural properties that are amenable to formalization and thereby to throw light on the theoretical limit of such particular aspects. This capacity is related to the extra-empirical aspects of the domain, and has therefore limited empirical impacts and consequences for the theory. Indeed, we may have to deliberately separate these formal studies from the question of empirical relevance, particularly in those cases where the validity of these studies can be justified only by ignoring the empirical context of the issues in question. And we can do so only by denying the problem of subsumption of qualitative variations by the formal concepts thus employed. In other words, we obtain transparency of structure by divorcing it from its field of application.

The Negative Effects of Formalization: Theory Metamorphosis

In many cases, formalization in social sciences is likely to yield the unintended consequence of handicapping, disrupting and significantly obstructing progress in knowledge. This springs chiefly from the fact that the reconstitution of a social science theory through the application of the formal method is likely to result in substantially altering the original theory. This is plausible because the theoretical constructs on which formalization relies upon are likely to capture only limited aspects of the original concepts and relations, and are thus incomplete representation of the human reality. Such incompleteness is caused in part by the fact that not all essential aspects of the original concepts are formalizable. Even if these essential aspects happen to be all captured, they may not be equally amenable to the same mode of formalization. That is, the same formalization may not be effectively or even consistently applied to all essential aspects of the original theory. This being the case, the resulting formalization may have missed significant properties or relations that are either essential to the original concepts, or that have contributed significantly to the overall property of the original concepts but whose contributions are rather obscure and difficult to articulate. The result of such incompleteness and the ensuing lopsided or misplaced representation mean that the original structure is no longer faithfully reproduced under the formal address. The formal model that results cannot be taken as a more precise representation of the original structure. It is just a different theory altogether.[4] We can call this particular type of theory change "theory metamorphosis."

Theory metamorphosis can occur along different routes. Where the reconstitution proceeds towards the trimming of empirical content in an attempt to clarify broader structural relations of the original theory through the imposition of the syntactical properties of a formal structure, the original theory is likely to be modified towards a more abstract and general level, taking on the characteristics of the formal model which shapes or guides its metamorphosis. At the extreme, it may develop into nothing more than a quasi-mathematical theory.

Theory metamorphosis may also result from researches directed towards studying the theoretical limits of an established domain. The study of theoretical limits requires as its pre-requisite the recasting of concepts into extremity forms and correspondingly, the making of extremity assumptions about its basic postulates.[5] While these extremity assumptions are useful for such restricted purpose, indiscriminate use of them may unwittingly lead to the dangerous result of theory metamorphosis. This can still be the case even where some of these extremity assumptions are retained but are partially relaxed for the building of other related models. The end product of such studies would be merely the articulation of theoretical limits upon certain aspects of the extremity assumptions of the first order. These second or third-order theoretical limits, no longer describing the broad shape of the established domain nor talking about the real world, become increasingly alienated from the original framework.

Even in the absence of reconstitution, theory metamorphosis may still take place as a domain grows bigger and as the relation between the core of the domain over its peripheral developments loosens. As a result, it becomes relatively easy for the periphery of the domain to interface with other domains and to partake the characteristics of these outside domains. Similarly, as a maturing domain is exhausting its development potentials, the practising researchers are inclined to look for growth possibilities by way of merging with affiliated domains or borrowing from them research frameworks or analytical tools. In addition, as a domain expands and as the stakes of the practising members in the very domain grow, it is also natural for them to institute ways to shield the domain or at least its core from being falsified. Unwittingly, such an orientation towards falsification aversion opens an opportunity for theory metamorphosis. Thus in a variety of ways, some degree of metamorphosis is likely to occur as a domain grows and develops.

With these possibilities, we can perhaps venture to postulate that there is an inherent inevitability for a growing domain to undergo some degree of metamorphosis. Even if the domain in question is completely free from the need to modify itself as a result of testing, even if it is not pushed to expand beyond its natural bounds, there is still the need to reconstitute the growing domain for cognitive clarity. And as long as there exists the need for reconstitution for one reason or another, it is difficult to prevent the development of a "reconstitution bias," for it would be unreasonable to expect the reconstituted theories to remain indefinitely isomorphic with the original theory. And even if the first reconstituted theory is a faithful representation of the original, it is unlikely that later reconstituted theories of a higher order will be so. And the more the number of times an original theory is reconstituted, the more magnified the reconstitution bias is likely to be.

Wholesale Metamorphosis

What causes problem is, however, not theory metamorphosis as such, for a reconstituted theory may prove to be of better explanatory power and less susceptible to error than the original counterpart. In this case, theory metamorphosis may be called progressive and the reconstitution represents progress in knowledge. Metamorphosis which takes place at the periphery and which does not represent any significant gain in knowledge is also natural and commonplace, for given man's cognitive limitations, it should not be counted as an epistemic ideal for the core of a domain to hold perfect control over what happens at the periphery.[6] Even metamorphosis at the periphery representing a distortion of the core in a degenerative sense should not be cause for alarm, as long as it is in principle correctable and non-epidemic. What really causes concern is metamorphosis taking place on a wholesale scale and in a degenerative manner. Degeneration can be defined in this regard partly in terms of the extent to which the reconstituted theory and its subsequent versions proceed along the line of misrepresenting or distorting the original theory and partly in terms of the extent it bars the realization of the epistemic potentials of the original theory in explaining the real world.

Some domains, as can be expected, are more susceptible to wholesale metamorphosis. Domains whose core concepts are by nature difficult to pin down are more open to a variety of interpretations and reconstitution possibilities. Similarly, a domain whose core as a whole is not well-developed, whose relations between its core concepts and the periphery are not well-defined, naturally allows more room for reconstitution. As can be expected, social science theories are more liable to share these characteristics than physical science theories. One common route to correct such looseness or sloppiness, as practised by social scientists, is the adoption of the formal method, in the strong belief that formal or mathematical precisification provides the most effective, if not the only way to make up for these deficiencies.[7] Little do they know that formalization as a tool of reconstitution is liable to bring about consequences entirely beyond their intention. Unaware of the problem of qualitative subsumption on the one hand and of the possibility that formal reconstitution of an ill-developed structure is liable to result in drastic alteration of the original theory on the other, social scientists in their earnestness to ape physical sciences almost abandon the most appropriate route of making up for the natural looseness of social science concepts through qualitative precisification, especially by way of working out and elaborating systematically significant gradations along the polarities of these concepts. Instead they work invariably along the route of formal or quantitative precisification, thus opening their theories to the possibility of theory metamorphosis on a wholesale scale.

The Nature and Role of Epistemic Archetypes

The development towards wholesale metamorphosis is often catalyzed and activated by a continuous interface between the existing domain and certain popular epistemic meta-patterns that serve to standardize interpretation of empirical content or data. These meta-patterns, acting as some kind of "idea pigeon-holes," cut across multiple disciplines and can readily fit into even divergent empirical data or evidences by virtue of their relatively high level of abstraction and generality, as well as their open-endedness in their mapping with other domains. We can call these meta-patterns *"epistemic archetypes."*[8]

From an epistemic viewpoint, there is more to an epistemic archetype than being a meta-pattern or thema in the sense that it manages to capture the structural properties of a wide array of empirical contents. An epistemic archetype also includes in its domain a kit of organizing, operating or generative principles which provide the heuristics to problem formation and solution. Thus on the one hand, it contains pseudo-empirical concepts and law-like statements, whose variables can be mapped into a variety of domains of lower levels. As such, it seems to command immense explanatory power. On the other hand, it can be likened to a tool box with a standard set of analytical apparatus and formal tools. Indeed an epistemic archetype is even more than just a simple or random combination of these themes and tools. It is a systematic package of organized interfaces and taxonomies between such themes and tools. Thus, it is capable of conferring structure to any domain, of standardizing what problems to formulate, how they should be formulated, and of systematizing how problems are to be appraised and solved. It is these thorough-going standardizing and heuristics-giving properties that characterize an epistemic archetype and give it formidable academic influences.

The epistemic archetype is useful in multiple ways to a growing domain which seeks to reflect on its own structure, which seeks to expand its boundary and which seeks to reconstitute itself for cognitive clarity or precision. An epistemic archetype provides a stepping stone, albeit a potentially dangerous one, for organized development and for structure elucidation. Through interfacing with its high power and abstract structure, a developing domain is able to grow in the most efficient and economical manner. In physics, the theme of hierarchy provides a typical example of an epistemic archetype. This is best illustrated by Holton (1978, 1981) who draws upon the attempts of physicists to give order to the bewildering variety of elementary particles via the theme of hierarchy, which acts as an organizing principle to create order out of chaos. Themes like conservation, equilibrium, evolution, dialectic are important examples of epistemic archetypes which find their presence over a wide range of disciplines.[9]

The evolution archetype is a case in point. Its influence is manifested not only in say, its direct descendants, e.g., Social Darwinism. Even in more remote areas, e.g., models of growth of knowledge, its influence is highly pervasive. The computer archetype is another important example. Its influence cuts across multiple disciplines and in the area of cognitive science, it almost dominates the entire field until very recently, with the advent of the brain metaphor. To a similar extent, the dialectic archetype is dominant in a multiplicity of social and political ideas and theories.

Beyond a point, the virtues of a domain interfacing with an epistemic archetype, however, turn out to be a curse in disguise. When researchers of a domain have habituated themselves to standardizing problems and solutions following the dictates of an epistemic archetype, wholesale metamorphosis will gradually take place as the original domain is being entirely reorganized, reinterpreted and reconstituted under the standardizing power of the archetype. In time, it is no longer the case that a particular domain sensibly borrows the insights from an epistemic archetype. It becomes in effect the case of how an epistemic archetype alters the original theory, colonizes the domain, and bars the production of genuine knowledge. Through continual reinterpretation of the original domain in terms of an archetype's vocabulary, taxonomy, and models, a wholesale theory metamorphosis may finally result leading to the exclusive production of pseudo-knowledge alien to the original "spirit" of the original domain. In some cases, this will also lead to the blending of pseudo-knowledge with genuine knowledge. And the more a domain has undergone metamorphosis, the more difficult it will be to distinguish what would be genuine knowledge from what is not.

Intensive assimilation of a particular domain by an epistemic archetype will in time reduce the effectiveness of attempts of falsification, both in the case where the theory metamorphosis develops towards a more abstract level or towards the existentialization of a general formula, a point that has been elaborated in Chapter Two. In the former case, it becomes more difficult for effective falsification to be formulated, while in the latter case, the stock of potential falsifiers becomes so enlarged that it becomes meaningless to apply them. This will develop to the point where falsification will be dropped altogether. Taking its place is the degenerative confirmatory approach, particularly in the manner of searching the best fit between data and theory.[10] This approach is degenerative because it allows or even positively encourages manipulation of data to fit the theory that had undergone metamorphosis. Together, such developments, i.e., standardization of interpretation of reality and orientation away from falsification, create the most damaging effect of all on the domain in question. Under the tyranny of the archetype, the domain undergoes a degenerative process. In time it will become divorced from reality. The reconstituted domain finally turns out to be only a manifesting prototype of an epistemic archetype.

NOTES

1. Even Carl Hempel, philosopher of science in the logical positivist tradition, has warned philosophers not to overrate "the importance of formalization, including axiomatization, as essential to proper scientific procedure" (Hempel, 1977).
2. "Physics defines itself as the science devoted to discovering, developing and refining those aspects of reality that are amenable to mathematical analysis.... Consider the typical subject matter and concepts of physics. Atoms and electrons provide us with identical distinct countable objects. Space and time approximate to continuous variables. Mass and charge are found to be invariant or conserved parameters. Stars and crystals are simple geometrical forms. Velocity and force are linear vector quantities. Electronics and magnetism are vector fields. Planets and stars are weakly interacting systems — and so on. All these qualities, which we think of as fortunately provided by nature for our better comprehension of its glories, have been selected by us, in order that we make some progress in representing them in terms of ideal models" (Ziman, 1978, pp.28-29).
3. "We are very far from being able to predict, even in physics, the precise results of a *concrete* situation, such as a thunderstorm, or a fire" (Popper, 1957, p.139).

4. The resulting formal theory might deviate from the informal theory so much that it could not plausibly be construed as being a reformulation of that theory. Rather it would be a different theory which displayed a certain similarity to the original informal theory. And being so precise, it would be significantly less well supported by the known facts than the vaguer informal theory (Suppe, 1977). Cf. also Loasby, "The process of model-building, in whatever field, goes beyond the decomposition of complexity. It involves the transformation of a set of phenomena into a form which is amenable to treatment by the techniques available. Transformation implies distortion; those who like to talk of mapping problems onto techniques may be reminded of the difficulty of mapping the globe (let alone the heavens) onto a flat sheet of paper" (Loasby, 1976, p.35).

5. For instance, the postulate of perfect information or perfect rationality.

6. The ultimate ideal is, of course, maximal correspondence with minimal building material.

7. Theory metamorphosis may take the informal (as opposed to the formal) route, such as the developments of Marxism.

8. Cf. Philip Pomper's notion of architectonic and how he applied it to the field of psychohistory. See Pomper (1985).

9. Holton also includes those notions like symmetry, continuum.

10. Econometrics is an area typical of the search for fit between data and theory.

Chapter Five
The Equilibrium Archetype and
the Equilibriumization of Economics

The Application of Epistemic Archetypes in Economics

It would be naive to assume that a scientific domain can develop in the absence of the influence of the prevailing epistemic archetypes. The key question for the academician is therefore how to make the best use of such archetypes, while at the same time taking measures to fend off colonization by any of them. In the case of a social science theory, this may include the development of a methodology tailored to its peculiar characteristics, the avoidance of lopsided reliance on any particular archetype, the development of objective criteria on the one hand and the nurture of a sensitivity on the other in determining the point beyond which continual application of a particular archetype will lead to degeneration. One such criterion would be whether or not the application of an archetype would result in the discovery of deeper albeit non-syntactical relations between the concepts within a domain or whether the continual application would lead to the cutting off of further discoveries of such non-syntactical complexities. The development of economic thought, viewed from such a perspective, provides an illuminating example of how the various domains within the discipline fall prey to the dominating archetype, the *equilibrium archetype*. Such a perspective helps also to reveal how economics has subsequently undergone a long degenerative process of theory metamorphosis to the point where the discipline as a whole could be described as being *"equilibriumized."*

The equilibrium archetype is of course not the only epistemic archetype that influences economic thought, but since it is most conducive to formal reconstitution, it is by far the most powerful and dominating. There is for instance the evolution archetype espoused by Boulding and some others who argue that the economic world is like an ecological system and that the relations between competitors resemble biological competition. Boulding's *Evolutionary Economics* is almost, as a matter of fact, a point-by-point mapping of the evolution domain with the economic domain. There is the entropy archetype espoused in the work of Georgescu-Roegen whose *The Entropy Law and Economic Progress* tries to represent economic progress by a system of equations explicitly modelled on those of thermodynamics. Towards a similar pattern is the effort of Albin's work *The Analysis of Complex Socioeconomic Systems,* which attempts to draw parallels between the economic order and the computer. And of course the long-standing dialectic archetype continues to haunt Marxian economics and its descendent, radical economics. The above archetypes, well-established or budding alike, have however only very limited influence on mainstream economics, which is almost exclusively dominated by the equilibrium archetype.

The Notion of Equilibrium and Self-equilibriability

Theorizing in terms of equilibrium in economics is by no means objectionable in itself. The notion of equilibrium itself and even the corresponding well-organized equilibrium archetype are both highly congenial to the study of economics. Many fundamental questions that could be raised or framed in economics have to do with the very idea of equilibrium, and in many instances, the formulation of an economic problem can be fruitfully achieved under the heuristics of equilibrium thinking.[1] The equilibrium archetype that prevails in economics stems by and large from Newtonian mechanics and celestial movements, but the question of origin can be immaterial to its applications and its subsequent colonization of economics.

The central question implicit in Adam Smith's *The Wealth of Nations* can in an enlightening way be conceived to be a question of equilibrium. His positive answer to the question of whether an economic world of decentralized individuals acting to promote their respective personal interests can result in a harmonious order can be given a fruitful equilibrium interpretation, although it needs to be qualified that the Smithian equilibrium vision is essentially a non-stationary one and that the equilibrium notion does not exhaust the Smithian vision. In the same vein, the Keynesian question of whether an economy, left to itself, is self-equilibrating, and thereby does not require government action to stabilize its operations, is essentially an equilibrium question. In both cases, the central notion that threads through them is the notion of self-equilibriability of a decentralized system, be it the economy in general or any market in particular. Each of these two questions, framed in terms of the self-equilibriability notion, is capable of opening up an entire domain for fruitful economic enquiry.

But the pursuit of this notion of equilibriability need not result in research programs as those being pursued in modern-day mainstream economics. The same notion might have been explored in alternative research programs that are, in spirit or in method, very different from what has actually been followed or practised in the discipline. A fruitful research program may have been the exploration of various stabilizing and destabilizing factors, agents, forces, processes, etc., that contribute to the equilibrating or disequilibrating movements of a decentralized economic system. These stabilizing or destabilizing factors may be structural features internal to the system or exogenous factors to the system, or they may represent their interacting resultants. Alternatively put, the question may be framed as to what features an economy must

possess such that it is self-equilibrating or that it becomes susceptible to disequilibrating movements. Corollarily, it may be asked at
what stage of development an economy would come to acquire certain characteristics that render it vulnerable to disequilibrating
forces. If so, what types of government action would be needed to
bring balance to the effects of these destabilizers and thereby what
characteristics these actions must partake in order to be effective at
some particular phase of development.

In more specific terms, such a research program may constitute
answers to the question as to how far the scale of an economy would
be crucial to the development of destabilizers. Research could also
be oriented towards the relations between ownership and management structures and their impacts on the stability of a particular
type of economy. A further important area of research, too, lies in
the stabilizing or destabilizing effects of technological changes and
perhaps also in how structural changes in consumer demand, for example, preferences towards consumer durables, snob goods or services, etc., contribute to the stability or instability of an economy.
Similarly, research could be directed to how far the money
economy, etc., is more prone to the development of destabilizing
processes. These questions could be asked independently or they
could be cross-examined from a multiplicity of viewpoints. Answers
to these questions would constitute not only a major research program that helps to throw light on the deeper mechanisms or structural properties about the operation of any economy. More important, the questions framed in this open-ended manner are capable
of capturing answers that take into account the dynamic dimensions
of an economy and of generating answers to accommodate unexpected changes or hitherto unforeseen developments of an
economy. Domains that are being generated along this direction
would thus provide sensible and realistic guidelines with respect to
what would be the most appropriate stabilizers a government should
adopt in order to counter-balance the destabilizing effects specific
to a particular economy at a particular phase of development.

From Equilibriability to General Equilibrium: Theory Metamorphosis in Micro-Economics

Mainstream economics, however, has not followed this mode of enquiry. It has instead steered economics away from this original notion of self-equilibriability in favor of a technical and fossilized representation of the state of equilibrium and of the search for ideal mathematical conditions that guarantee the existence of equilibrium in an economy. A kind of theory metamorphosis on a wholesale scale, transforming the fundamental research programs of economics both in the realm of micro- and macro-economics, has led to the almost complete equilibriumization of economics, as can be witnessed in the history of economics.[2]

In micro-economics, the Smithian concern for harmony in a decentralized world of individual actions was gradually shifted towards equilibrium thinking under the Ricardian deductive methodology.[3] The marginal revolution, which paved the way for the Marshallian partial equilibrium, resulted in a standard point of departure for formal analysis in terms of maximizing a mathematical function under constraints (Pasinetti, 1981, p.10). This in turn prepared the ground for a full shift of focus to the question of how to systematically represent an economy in equilibrium. The shift culminated in an elegant formal expression by Walras who suggested that maximizing behavior under certain conditions would result in general market equilibrium. In his hand, the question of the equilibrium of an economy was changed to a representational problem in algebraic terms and to a problem of finding a unique mathematical solution to this representation. Subsequent developments in micro-economics, taking this as another standard point of departure, engaged themselves by and large in the exploration of new modes of mathematical representation of the economy in equilibrium, and of explicating the mathematical properties (e.g. the stability, determinacy) of such mathematically represented equilibrium systems. The standard problems confronting the researcher become the proving of the existence of an equilibrium, and the determining of the equilibrium values and conditions in a stationary state.

While Walras's *Pure Economics* was crude by modern mathematical standard,[4] his representation was refined decades later by Wald, who demonstrated the existence of a competitive equilibrium with mathematical rigor in 1936. Then, Neumann (1937) gave it a thrust and the existence of a dynamic competitive equilibrium path was mathematically established.

Much reconstitution of the domain then followed with substantial additions and elaborations. For instance, Samuelson (1941) provided the taxonomy of stability and equilibria and the conditions for stability of equilibrium through the exposition of mathematical properties; Hicks (1939) tied behavioral assumptions to market supply and demand relations in an optimization theory; Smithies (1942) gave economic meaning to the mathematical version of stability conditions; and Metzler (1945) unified Samuelson's and Hicks's different formulations by demonstrating their equivalence.

The general equilibrium (GE) research program reached a new platform by Arrow and Debreu (1954) who introduced production sets and preference structures to GE theory to re-phrase the problem of competitive equilibrium. Kakutani's fixed-point theorem was used by McKenzie (1954) and Brouwer's fixed-point theorem was used by Gale (1955) to achieve the same result, i.e., proving the existence of a competitive equilibrium. Present-day general equilibrium analysis is by and large an extension of the Arrow-Debreu framework to incorporate uncertainty (Radner), information (Fisher, Diamond, etc.), transaction cost (Hahn, Kurz, etc.), money (Grandmont and Younes), technological change (Makarov), and so forth.[5]

In the 60's, GE was mostly rewritten from a game-theoretic perspective. Itself a powerful epistemic archetype, the game theory is applicable to a wide range of disciplines in social sciences. In the realm of economics, it has rendered support to the equilibrium archetype by providing a taxonomy of strategies that can be adopted by the individual in his relations with others, and by corollary, a taxonomy of conflict or cooperative situations among them. These strategies and situations can be mapped to the decisions and behaviors of the rational economic man and correspondingly, to economic situations and systems. Following Nash's Bargaining Theory and Neumann and Morgenstern's Game Theory, GE was reinterpreted as an n-person cooperative game, in which an equilibrium outcome is defined as one that cannot be further improved upon by the formation or dissolution of any coalition. Starting from the maximizing motive of the rational economic man, game theory spells out formally the intricacies of how economic agents are supposed to interact with one another, how they voluntarily form or dissolve coalition to arrive at the equilibrium outcome, and how they optimize and allocate payoffs in the core solution set. By lending strong support to the equilibrium archetype, the game archetype has thus been playing a crucial role in the equilibriumization of economics.[6]

These developments, rigorous and sophisticated as they were, have failed to take into account an important methodological consideration, namely, the isomorphism between mathematics and economic reality. The validity of the approach of existence proof and of the determination of equilibrium values, it has to be recognized, rests solely on the unquestioned assumption of the truthfulness of representation of an economy by mathematical tools. In other words, the validity of existence proof and the subsequent search for equilibrium values are contingent upon and relative to the isomorphism of relations between the real world and the set of mathematical equations. Such isomorphism, even in broad terms, is missing in the most rigorous of representations. This should be obvious if we consider that with the advent of large corporation, big government, modern technology, the increased lead time in the production of producer goods, etc., a large part of economic phenomena in the modern economies as we know of is far-from-equilibrium. What mathematical systems set out to represent are only those variables which are observable or measurable, and which thereby come rather late in the causal sequences in the chain of economic events. The non-observable and non-measurable factors that really matter, that causally contribute to the stabilizing or destabilizing processes of the economy, e.g., the human motivation that underpins every economic system, the entrepreneurship that leads to risk-taking investments, the visions of a promising future that goads human efforts, etc. are *de facto* excluded from the wholesale application of formal tools. With such exclusion, whatever isomorphism that can be attained would be surface relations. And without structured isomorphism as opposed to surface isomorphism or the methodological backup to approach some kind of structured isomorphism, such mathematical efforts become merely academic exercises. Not only do they themselves fail to become genuine knowledge in economics, but they have also obstructed the acquisition or production of genuine knowledge. The production function, for instance, has to be assumed linear and homogeneous because there is only one type of mathematical function that enables marginal productivities to be actually equated to factor prices, so that they could be freely substituted for the factor prices without affecting the total net product that has to be appropriated without leaving any residual, positive or negative (Pasinetti, 1981, p.15).

Game theory is a case in point. When the theory is extended from a 2-person to an n-person game and from a non-cooperative to a cooperative one, it appears to have increased its representation power to account for the competitive market through exhausting the logical possibilities and probabilities of outcome of cooperation and conflict between rational economic agents. By applying set theory, probability theory and adding risk aversion assumption, side-payment concept, etc., game theory goes as far as perfect rationality allows. But the formal properties developed under its framework, which are essentially mathematical properties of a "pseudo-maximum problem," are neither isomorphic with the structural properties of an economy nor with the cognitive properties of a true human being. While game theory vigorously explores the cognitive strengths of the economic man — how a rational calculating mind translates a maximizing motive into optimal economic gain through anticipating and taking rational strategies — it does not and cannot take into account the cognitive weaknesses of the real human being which characterize economic actions and decisions. Similarly, while the game archetype is applicable to many types of human and economic situations, it is by no means capable of exhausting all important economic situations. Economic growth, for instance, which represents the result of the individual abstaining from his current consumption, of investing heavily in a future that promises by upgrading his capabilities and of scanning opportunity signals from events that happen around him, need not fall within the purview of the game archetype. Thus, game theorizing in economics can at best yield the theoretical limits of what a group of "super-rational" market participants would achieve under extremity assumptions, such as complete, transitive, reflexive and continuous preference relations, ordinal utility indexing to outcomes, full information about all preference relations, etc. All in all, it is a branch of mathematics that can contribute only marginally to the production of genuine knowledge in economics.[7]

Macro-equilibriability and Theory Metamorphosis in Macro-Economics

A more or less parallel situation has developed in macro-economics. The fundamental and well-meaning Keynesian proposition that the capitalist economy is incapable of self-equilibrating and thereby needs intervention from the government was recast in the neo-classical equilibrium framework. What Keynes outlined in his *General Theory* was the macro-consequences of the dynamic forces working in a decentralized economy. Keynes never lost sight of the disequilibrating factors at work, such as uncertain expectations, "intended savings" versus "desired consumption" and so on. He analyzed the interplay between these elements and disputed the then conventional wisdom of equilibria in all markets. In fact,

Keynes took equilibrium as a hypothetical notion that may never be realized. His analysis has more to do with how an economy oscillates between equilibrium states and how it is subject to disequilibrium movements.

Keynes's insights were selectively adopted and interpreted by Hicks and popularized by Samuelson. From his Walrasian background, Hicks reinterpreted Keynes's theory of interest rate and equilibriumized it in the IS-LM model. Investment and savings, income and interest, were paired together to illustrate the possibility of equilibrium in all markets. Hansen and Samuelson provided the 45-degree "Keynesian Cross" to further demonstrate the existence of national income equilibrium. Inflationary and deflationary gap are said to exist when the economy is not in equilibrium. Such a line of enquiry leads to the search of equilibrium values instead of discovering further the forces at work in an economy and their macro-consequences. What would have therefore been a most fruitful research program of the self-equilibriability of an economy as a whole was reduced into a special case of neo-classical equilibrium economics. Subsequent research problems become standardized into the determination of the equilibrium values of output and employment of an economy and thereby of how these values can be realized with or without government action.

With the core of micro-economics being re-written from the GE perspective and the synthesis of the Keynesian macro-equilibriability question into the neo-classical equilibrium framework, the major metamorphosis in economic thought becomes firmly entrenched. The subsequent course of development represents ñot much more than a point by point interpretation of economics in terms of the equilibrium archetype, or in short, the equilibriumization of economics.

Consequences of Equilibriumization in Economics

That present-day economics is thus not the fruitful use and intelligent application of the equilibrium concept, but rather the result of a systematic colonization of the equilibrium archetype, needs to be further substantiated. Proofs of "equilibriumization" can be established in both the methodological and the substantive realms. On the methodological front, several important features stand out that clearly characterize the development of equilibriumization. First the "ontology" of economic concepts becomes almost completely equilibriumized; that is, for every major economic concept that exists in the economic literature, there now exists an equilibriumized version. Key concepts such as growth, efficiency, competition, etc. have their distinctly equilibriumized counterparts which differ very substantially from what these concepts first signified or what could be conceived from the commonsense standpoint. Even the concept innovation was equilibriumized within the context of an extended version of the Arrow-Debreu model. This MN Model (Makarov, 1976), for instance, says nothing about the nature and process of innovation. It merely asserts the existence of equilibrium through a mathematical representation, first subsuming the inputs of innovation as "resources vector" for the purpose of deriving a new production set that encompasses in principle the production of innovation, and then turning them into "boolean vector" for the realization of a certain production set that includes the production of innovations. Such senseless representation can never explain how innovation comes about, let alone how it relates to a real economy.

Another typical example of how an originally rich concept was recast into a sterile equilibrium version is the concept of conspicuous consumption. When Veblen analyzed the practice of consumption and the formation of tastes (Veblen, 1899), he meant to argue that consumption patterns and tastes are the essential parts of the economic process and that assigning utility function to individuals is irrelevant and futile. According to Veblen, conspicuous consumption is an ultimate expression of pecuniary strength rather than that of utility maximization. But Veblen's idea was later turned into "conspicuous consumption utility function," represented by "expected conspicuous price," which results in equilibrium in a perfect market under perfect information.[8]

A second methodological implication of equilibriumization is the tacit assumption that all economic phenomena are either equilibriumizable or in those rare cases where they are not, they can be captured by the negation of equilibrium, i.e. disequilibrium. In other words, all economic phenomena of necessity fall within the broad purview of equilibrium and its negation, disequilibrium. Under this "pan-equilibrium" vantage point, all economic phenomena have to be and can be analyzed only within the equilibrium framework. To the minority economists, in particular the Post-Keynesians, disequilibrium has been sensibly used to denote the destabilizing factors and dynamic processes that characterize the capitalist economy, such as the mutual adaptation and confrontation among firms, the pricing of goods, the fixing and changing of wages, the conflicting forces that drive prices and wages away from equilibrium, etc.[9] In a similar vein, the Austrian School interprets equilibrium conditions as states giving the direction towards which the free market would approach but would never be able to reach. Economic analysis in its view should therefore be focused on adjustment processes instead of the final states of equilibrium. But to many equilibrium theorists, disequilibrium is a merely reconciliatory expedient employed to reconstitute the disequilibrating concepts within the equilibrium framework. Under this pan-equilibrium strategy, Keynes's original concerns of market instability, of the devastating state of unemployment, become comfortably incorporated in the name of disequilibrium and become logical derivatives of the equilibrium theory. The subsequent development of the branch of "disequilibrium economics" is a clear demonstration of this methodological bias.

With respect to the handling of an economic problem, the equilibrium archetype dictates standardized ways of formulating, formalizing, and of appraising the problem in question. The problem is first re-cast in an equilibrium model, to be followed by the determination of values and conditions under which an equilibrium exists or takes place. Or else the question is one of whether a postulated situation is consistent with equilibrium, i.e., it will produce an eventual outcome in which all plans are fulfilled and outcomes consistent, so that there is no further tendency to change.[10] In other words, each economic problem is phrased in such a manner that an equilibrium state is a nexus in which certain conditions are satisfied (Loasby). The decision or policy question that follows such a formulation becomes inescapably that of maximization and optimalization. Such standardized methods are usually followed with the utmost faith as if no other route of enquiry is conceivable.[11] The same influence of this stereotyped equilibrium methodology prevails with respect to the introduction of new variables to an existing model, or of adding new range of values to existing variables. In contrast to the dogged adherence to problem formulation in terms of the equilibrium model, the introduction of complications to a model is often made on a selective, non-systematic, and sometimes random basis. The unquestioned acceptance of the equilibrium approach cuts off *de facto* the application and development of potentially competing alternatives on a systematic basis. This tacit commitment to the equilibrium modelling thus smothers the ingenuity in taking a fresh perspective in problem formulation.

The equilibrium archetype not only dictates specific methods of problem formulation and appraisal, but it also provides a kind of "meta" heuristics to the development of new research programs. By ways of example, it may be pointed out what are looked upon as innovative research programs in economics such as the human capital school developed by Schultz and Becker, or the rational expectation school espoused by Muth and Lucas, etc., depend invariably and crucially on both the world view and the method supplied by the equilibrium archetype in spite of the obvious possibility that both human capital and economic expectation can be richly and realistically explored from perspectives other than the equilibrium viewpoint.

With the equilibriumization of economics, rigor and precision now rank as the most important ideals, the ranking being openly endorsed by leading members of the profession.[12] Depth of understanding and explanatory power of real world affairs give way as only matters of secondary importance. With this orientation, falsification as a method comes to point of abandonment, though lip service may still being paid to it as an ideal.[13] Instead, the merit of a model is appraised on how well it fits certain empirical data.

The Tyranny of the Equilibrium Archetype

On the substantive front, the tyranny of the equilibrium archetype is manifested in its suppression of other viable research programs that may pose a potential threat to its status. The phenomenon of increasing returns is a paradigmatic example. Increasing returns, which is a prevalent fact in economic life and a crucial link between economic organization and growth, is denied of any theoretical significance in mainstream economic analysis. Acceptance of the significance of increasing returns would surely open up an entirely new and a most pregnant research program in economic enquiry.[14] It would imply the injection of the effects of learning, the elevation of the role of accumulation of human capital, and the emphasis on the importance of institutional arrangements and managerial know-how. Equally important, the acceptance of increasing returns would be pointing to the acceptance of room for innovation at all levels and scales of economic activities, and with this, to the possibilities of exploring their rich relations with technological development a factor that has long been brushed aside as an exogenous factor to equilibrium analysis. The acceptance of this series of new variables and relations would be pointing to a new economics with its self-propelling dynamics, a new research program that is more true-to-life and thereby would surely pose a threat to the hegemony of equilibrium analysis. The stakes being too high for equilibrium theorists, increasing returns must therefore be ignored and suppressed.

In a similarly tyrannical manner, the equilibrium archetype reigns over nearly every major sector of economics. For instance, almost the whole domain of welfare economics is dominated by the equilibrium archetype. And to different degrees are the subjects of money, trade, growth and development.[15] The equilibriumization of economic growth is particularly illuminating. Under the regime of the equilibrium archetype, growth is characterized as a succession of a series of equilibrium points which constitute the growth path of an economy. Here again, the chief research problem is to determine the values and conditions under which such equilibrium points can be materialized. Institutional factors and changes which promote or pose as barriers to growth are simply assumed away or considered to be invariants in the very process. Selective injection of new variables into or modification of existing variables within these models, yielding at best a taxonomy of interesting cases, is invariably conceived as the only and probably the most respectable route of progress in the subject. The richness and diversity of real world factors and mechanisms, whose interplay provides the basis for growth and development is almost completely ignored. Even the most innovative contributions to economic theory in relation to the problem of production that Pasinetti has in his mind, i.e., Kalecki's theory of unemployment, Leontief's input-output analysis, Sraffa's production of commodities scheme, Harrod-Domar's macro-dynamic models, etc., theories that have escaped the cherished mathematical tool of maximization under constraint (Pasinetti, 1981, p. 17), nevertheless still fall within the gigantic shadow of the equilibrium archetype.

Similarly, equilibriumization has led to the subversion of many useful economic concepts and yielded strange concepts contrary to our commonsense ideas or experiences. Thus the concept of uncertainty is stripped of its openness to become "determinate" or "determinable" uncertainty. The concept of search is so distorted that the standard problem in this regard becomes one of determining "search equilibrium," in spite of the obvious fact that the notion of search is only remotely related to the notion of equilibrium. Even the phenomenon of prevailing fixed prices which is significantly at variance with the notion of equilibrium is being recklessly reinterpreted and studied within the framework of equilibrium under concepts like "fix-price equilibrium."

As economics evolves along the line of equilibrium, its hard core has grown into the study of equilibrium itself, rather than the study of economics. GE theorists are in fact exploring the formal structural properties of the equilibrium archetype rather than how equilibrating and disequilibrating forces in the real world are generated, how they converge and balance off each other, how a dynamic process develops, etc. Thus, Hahn has to admit that "GE is strong on equilibrium and very weak on how it comes about" (Hahn, 1973, p.327). This contrasts sharply to the Classical economic tradition, which is strong in economics and weak in equilibrium.

Present-day micro-economics should be more appropriately called "equilibriumics" instead of economics. It has retreated to the position of pure mathematical interest. It is not descriptive of the real world and it makes no causal claim (Hahn, 1973, p.7). This is necessarily so, because equilibrium economics is no longer a genuine branch of economics. In its merger with the equilibrium archetype, it has been uplifted to such abstract levels of discourse where real world affairs are not matter of its concern.[16] It is not surprising for Leontief to discover that more than half of the articles published in *American Economic Review* between 1972-1981 are "mathematical models without any data."[17] In fact, empirical data have a small role to play in academic exercises of this kind.

Intellectual "Schizophrenia"[18] in Economics

One significant consequence of the equilibriumization of economics is that economics is thrown into a state of "intellectual schizophrenia." As can be expected, different domains of economics experience varying rates of equilibriumization. The core of economics might be fully equilibriumized, but there are certain parts away from the core that remain less affected by the equilibrium archetype. This incompleteness can in part be attributed to the fact that in spite of the process of reconstitution, the original pre-reconstituted frameworks have nevertheless survived. And as the reconstituted theories drift away from reality, the original pre-reconstituted frameworks which were fundamentally rooted in reality may stand out and remain autonomous of the equilibriumization process. Similarly, equilibriumization is unlikely to replace or even encapsulate to a substantial degree the vast amount of economic commonsense or knowledge that grow out of pragmatic affairs of the real world. Thus, in spite of almost complete equilibriumization at the core, the periphery of the economics discipline is still pervaded by the world of commonsense, and to some lesser extent, the pre-reconstituted theories which are tied somehow crudely to the real world, and more probably to a combination of these elements. And as the core of economics is drawn away from reality towards the more abstract levels of analysis or discourse by the equilibrium archetype, the schism between the two worlds is likely to widen further.

Take Galbraith as an example. His work has always irritated mainstream economists, who find it hard to equilibrimize or incorporate his ideas comfortably into their framework. Galbraith's concept of producer sovereignty is not reconciliable with the neoclassical framework. His theory of the technostructure can hardly find an appropriate place in the neoclassical paradigm. His conception of the planning system, which he claims to exist side by side with the market system and has about the same size of the latter, is too not readily equilibriumizable. Intellectual schizophrenia in economics is most evident when Galbraith was left to himself to spell out the principles governing the operation of big corporations, to introduce political concepts into economics, etc., while mainstream economists never take him nor other like-minded economists seriously in their preoccupation with their equilibriumization of economics.[19]

Similarly, most of Joan Robinson's important contributions which bear a very different philosophical outlook are left aside because they are not amenable to equilibrium analysis. She believed that expectations about the future are shaped by past experience, and past decisions might have irreversible outcomes. As a result, history and time of necessity play an important role in determining the reactions of economic agents. In the realm of growth, she emphasized checks to growth, the inevitable imbalances and the inherent instability of the economic system. She raised problems regarding the measurement of capital, thereby challenging the legitimacy of the neoclassical aggregate production function. These ideas, being diametrically opposed to the equilibrium thinking, have, too, to be ignored.

The consequences of economics suffering from such a state of schizophrenia are obvious. First, big gaps can be observed between the levels of sophistication of high theories and their naivety in application to the real world. Loasby (1976, p.50), for instance, has noticed and pointed out the paradox of the various naive ways the most rigorous general equilibrium theory is put to explain the real world. This paradox of theorizing rigor and application naivety is thus an obvious symptom of schizophrenia that economics has been suffering from. Another interesting observation is that economists find that increasingly their empirical researches, for example, in the case of econometrics, become dissociated from the core economic theories (Klamer, 1983, p.243). Such dissociation, again, is anything but natural. To have pragmatic relevance, empirical researches have either to abandon as their guideline the core theory which has drifted away from the real world, or else they have to incorporate more and more economic commensense, filtered or unfiltered alike. In both cases, it is natural that these empirical researches take on the appearance that they are conducted independently of theories.

The Role of Formalization in Economics: A Concluding Remark

A logical question that may arise from the above analysis is whether or not economics would fare better if it comes under only the effects of formalization without the dominating influence of the idea of equilibrium. In other words, the question is whether or not we can separately appraise the effects of formalization on economics. Such an answer can, of course, hardly be obtained in any precise manner. We have already pointed out the inevitable development of "wholesale formalization" at the later stage of an epistemic cycle in the preceding chapter. Another development that economics will suffer from anyway and that can have serious repercussions on the discipline is "pre-mature formalization." This refers to the state whereby excess formalization occurs before a growing domain has the opportunity to become qualitatively precisified and before significant qualitative variations and relations have been captured by its coarse structure in the process of assimulating new empirical content.[20] Since the quality of a piece of formalization must of necessity depend on the quality and the fineness of the pre-formalized knowledge, pre-mature formalization might deprive the coarse structure of the opportunity to acquire straightaway significant empirical content. That is, the intermediate stage between the unfolding of a coarse structure and the formalization of its structural aspects is being short-circuited. Thus, even if economics were spared the influences of the equilibrium archetype, it can hardly escape from the joint effects of wholesale formalization and pre-mature formalization.[21]

A coherent picture can now be pieced together from the foregoing criticisms. The benefits of formalization to social sciences are far outweighed by its negative aspects. Formalization is a highly risky business, for it is difficult to keep it in within bounds without causing theory metamorphosis and difficult to avoid the existentialization or trivialization of a seemingly general formula. It is incapable of developing criteria to prevent itself from adopting false assumptions which harmfully distort reality. Both to extract the best out of formalization and to contain its vices require inevitably something beyond the formal skills, for such activities and skills themselves are autonomous of the formal method and are governed by non-formal factors and considerations. "Knowing how to carry out a sequence of analytical operations is not the same as knowing the appropriate domain of application, nor is it the same as knowing how to start and when to stop the sequence" (Rosen, 1980, p.3).

Formalization is difficult to apply risklessly, and it could be costly if a bad formalization results. Even when these hurdles are overcome, what formalization can contribute would still be very meagre, unimportant and uninteresting. In other words, formalization in the realm of social sciences is unable to promise much, pays very little, is very costly to conduct and very risky to contain. Thus, while formalization has revolutionized the development of the physical sciences, we may have come by now to a full circle, where we will find that revolutions in the social sciences have to await the abandonment of the formal method as the chief tool of enquiry.

NOTES

1. I am therefore not in entire agreement with the extreme though understandable criticisms of the notion of equilibrium found, for instance, in the writings of Wiseman. "Equilibrium is a fascinating intellectual toy. But it is irrelevant to the real problems of economics, and should be dropped from our vocabulary" (Wiseman, 1983, p.23).

2. This is in spirit congenial to the idea of "marginalization" of economics conceived by Pasinetti (1981, p.18).

3. Kaldor, however, identified the source of error with the middle of the fourth chapter of Vol. I of *The Wealth of Nations* where "Smith's interest gets bogged down in the question of how values and prices for products and factors are determined. One can trace a more or less continuous development of price theory from the subsequent chapters of Smith through Ricardo, Walras, Marshall right up to Debreu and the most sophisticated of present-day Americas" (1972, p.181).

4. Cf. Neumann and Morgenstern (1944, p.4).

5. For details, see Weintraub (1985). Also see Debreu (1985).

6. Ironically, when Neumann first formulated game theory, his interest was as much in mathematics as in economics, and his intention was to devise a theory of "game of strategy" to study the "pseudo-maximum problem" which has been "nowhere dealt with in classical mathematics" (p.11). In the same vein, Neumann and Morgenstern never claimed that game theory is the only way to study economic behavior, nor did they call for the equilibriumization of economics through this route. On the contrary, they are quite aware of the richness and multiplicity of economic phenomena and of the fact that game theory has the modest aim of examining "only some commonplace experience concerning human behavior which lends itself to mathematical treatment." In fact, they suspect that mathematical discoveries of a stature comparable to that of calculus — which makes possible Newton's creation of mechanics — will be needed in order to produce success in economics. It is therefore surprising that game theory with such "limited" use should be taken as a superior approach in economic theorizing in general and equilibrium analysis in particular.

7. This is congenial to Shackle's position on game theory: "...the Theory of Games...in reducing games or battles to a mathematical analysis, it was found necessary to grant, by supposition, to each contestant, a precise and guaranteed knowledge of what would be the consequence, the 'pay-off', of each possible pair of strategies, one strategy for each of them, that they might adopt. Thus the conduct of each was determined: he must reduce as far as possible the damage which his enemy could do him by choosing that strategy whose worst possible pay-off was, for him, the least bad of all such pay-offs. Thus surprise is ruled out..." (1972).

8. See Leibenstein, 1950.

9. Cf. Iwai, 1981.

10. See Wiseman (1983, p.23).

11. Thus, Debreu invented the concept "social equilibrium" and started out to prove its existence. Through his reformulation, Pareto optimum was dressed up as "valuation equilibrium." See Debreu (1983).

12. Including notably Samuelson.

13. See Blaug (1980, p.260).

14. "The consequences of abandoning the axiom of 'linearity' and assuming that, in general, the production of any one commodity, or any one group of commodities, is subject to increasing returns to scale, are very far-reaching. The first and most important casualty is the notion of 'general

equilibrium' as such. The very notion of 'general equilibrium' carries the implication that it is legitimate to assume that the operation of economic forces is constrained by a set of exogenous variables which are 'given' from the outside and stable over time. It assumes that economic forces operate in an environment that is 'imposed' on the system in a sense other than being just a heritage of the past—one could almost say an environment which, in its most significant characteristics, is independent of history. These critical exogenous features of the 'environment' include Pareto's 'tastes and obstacles'—the preferences of individuals as consumers, the transformation functions of factors into the products and the supply of resources—at any rate of 'ultimate resources'—which are thus transformed." (Kaldor, 1972).

15. Cf. Blaug (1968, p.588).
16. "Mathematical economics, by and large, does live and operate in a universe of its own, with little or no contact with the real world of economic events. It is said that most of the really great economists of the past have been nonmathematical ....." John Blatt, *How Economists misuse Mathematics,* in Eichner (1983, p.184).
17. *Science,* V.217, n.4555, July 9, 1982.
18. Not strictly following the standard meaning in psychology. I am indebted to Peter Earl for pointing this out.
19. Thus, Galbraith was treated as a "trivializing journalist" and was dismissed as "a superficial Mickey Mouse of scientific economics." See Canterbery, 1980, p.231.
20. It is manifest that the systematic interconnections among the concepts occurring in any of the following theories at present are insufficiently well known or understood to admit of fruitful axiomatization: Hebb's theory of the central nervous system, Darwin's theory of evolution, Hoyle's theory on the origin of the universe, Pike's tagmemic theory of language structure, Freud's psychology, Heyerdahl's theory about the origin of human life on Easter Island, or the theory that all Indo-European languages have a common ancestor language, proto-Indo-European. Furthermore, it is manifest that most theories in cultural anthropology; most sociological theories about the family; theories about the origin of the American Indian; most theories in paleontology; theories of phylogenetic descent; most theories in histology, cellular and microbiology, and comparative anatomy; natural history theories about the decline of the dinosaur and other prehistoric animals; and theories about the higher processes in psychology, all are such at present that any attempts at ax-

iomatization would be premature and fruitless since they are insufficiently developed to permit their reduction to a highly systematic basis in the manner described above which is required for fruitful axiomatization. Suppe (1977, p.65).

21. There is then in a significant sense, an inevitability of economics developing into the present state it is. Hence I cannot subscribe fully to Guy Routh's "contingency" thesis, namely, the hereditary characteristics of economic thought are much more pronounced than the environmental, and that history of economics would have taken an alternative course if it had been a different set of ideas and people to start with (Routh, 1975, p.295). That would be true only at the level of fairly specific contents.

Chapter Six
From a Cognitive Point of View

Formal Versus Natural Language

In the ultimate analysis, the issue of formalization can hardly be separated from the issue of the formal (or artificial) language versus the natural language and perhaps from the even broader context of man's cognitive capabilities and invariants. A discussion of these broader issues would enhance our understanding of the relative role and significance of the formal method employing the formal language.

It has first of all to be recognized that being man's cognitive tools, both the formal and the natural languages have their respective strengths and weaknesses. The formal language can be likened to a "logical machine" man invents and employs. For all its potential use and value, it is not meant to nor can by any means supplant completely man's natural intelligence and its adaptive properties which exist bountifully though sometimes confusingly in man's natural language.[1]

The formalization approach is cognitively significant because it strongly makes up for the limitations of man's "natural" cognitive apparatus. The formal machinery enables man to draw conclusions that lie far beyond his natural processing capabilities. It can be likened to a kind of "extra-sensory" organ that enables man to extend far beyond his ordinary and immediate intellectual senses. In removing ambiguities embedded in the natural language, it makes transparent essential structures, rendering them amenable to man's cognitive need for sharpness and clarity. It further satisfies man's cognitive need and criteria for economy and simplicity because skilful abstractions enable minimal premises to derive the most powerful of conclusions, and the right syntactical machinery can uncover the most hidden of them. Furthermore, the formal machinery ensuring neutral transmission of meaning or truth values, avoids the problems of logical inconsistency or internal contradictions. These properties are cognitively significant, for the human mind, limited in attention resources, processing capacity as well as retrieval capacity, has to depend heavily on an extra-sensory yet mechanical apparatus to discharge these functions more efficiently and effectively. The formal machinery which fills this gap beautifully can therefore be looked upon as an ideal and indeed a unique cognitive extension or accessory[2] of man.

Apart from guaranteeing consistency, detecting redundancy etc., a formalized system conveys the appearance of completeness. While this sense of completeness is not necessarily a cognitive virtue, and could in many cases constitutes a mere illusion, it does help man to punctuate his enquiries in a systematic manner.

Limitations of the Formal Language

In case we are carried away too far by the apparent power of the formal machine, let us, however, be reminded that the formal machine itself is by no means a flawless tool in its representation of nature or reality. Indeed, even the most rigorous formal structures in logic and mathematics have been shown to have definite limits (Gödel, Kleene, Turing, Tarski, Church, Löwenheim-Skolem). It has been demonstrated that a sufficiently rich formal theory cannot demonstrate its own non-contradictions nor the decidability of all its theorems in terms of its own system (Gödel). To do so, it requires the introduction of a stronger or a meta-system, *ad infinitum*. In other words, the laws of nature, and for that matter, the laws of human or social reality, cannot be formulated as an axiomatic, deductive, formal and unambiguous system which is also complete (Bronowski, 1977).

Like a machine, the formal language is by nature rigid and fairly inflexible. While it can fine-tune analytic results deductively, it has no synthesizing power to assimilate and reach out to the unforeseen and qualitatively distinct data once the formal machine has been set, and therein lies its rigidity. Thus it has little power to accommodate the diversities and the flux of the social and economic reality. Lopsided reliance on the formal language naturally leads us to "linear" reasoning (though not linear in the technical sense) and to the commitment of the induction bias. Functioning as an extra-sensory extension or accessory of human intelligence, the formal tool has encapsulated and deployed very effectively albeit only a limited aspect of man's overall cognitive techniques. But to give this limited aspect a disproportionately significant role and to expect this limited emphasis to yield the most and best of results is nothing less than courting the impossible. Hence wholesale formalism is bound to fail.

The Power of the Natural Language

Contrary to his formal language, man's natural language possesses several remarkable characteristics. First of all, the natural language is the real or true thinking tool of man. Man lives with two languages, an inner one and an outer one (Bronowski, 1977). The inner language which is entirely a natural language is his thinking language, with which he experiments new ideas or finds new arrangements of words or sentences that are more effective to convey his old ideas. By contrast, the outer language represents by and large the final output of his inner thinking experiments. The formal language which is part of his outer language is therefore not part and parcel of man's natural thinking apparatus. It is fundamentally an "operative" language that has no true thinking power nor reflective capacity.

As a corollary, man's inner language, and correspondingly his natural language, is essentially open, in the sense that its words are not unambiguously defined (Bronowski, 1977, p.118). The outer language which we all share is by comparison closed,[3] and this is particularly so in the case of the formal language which is a subset of the outer language. By definition, formal languages are incapable of recognizing themselves and are therefore also incapable of recognizing any other position. Thus, a formal language does not link positions, but constitutes itself a fixed position. It does not see the world beyond itself, only the world within itself. It is not, like philosophy, an open eye to the outer world, but a closed eye which may also be called a logically isolated eye (Pankow, 1976). Every formalization represents thus an act of closure, which in turn implies an imposition of restrictive conditions on the subject matter under study. "But the real world is never, at any moment, 'complete'. It is the open-endedness of our affairs, their unceasing natural and inherent engenderment of change which a model cannot accommodate. The model is spare, austere, arid. The world of experience is richly varied, inherently vague, restless and unexpected."[4]

Man's thinking language is not only an open system, but it is also an extremely rich and diverse system in terms of background knowledge and beliefs. It is this richness and diversity that enable man to detect signals and acquire new and probably unique insights into the external world of events. Such richness constitutes more or less a pre-requisite for the generation of useful pre-formalized knowledge, although no correlation between the degree of richness and the amount of useful pre-formalized knowledge can be or need to be assumed.[5] Just as the formation of useful formal knowledge depends crucially on the richness of the stock of pre-formalized knowledge,[6] the development of pre-formalized insights is, too, dependent on the richness of man's thinking language in the form of the natural language.

Another remarkable feature about man's natural language is that it is capable of at once being used synthetically and analytically. On the one hand, it can be used to analyze experience into parts; on the other hand, its parts can be subsequently being re-assembled into different imaginary constructions. It is this double activity of analysis and synthesis, a procedure which Bronowski called "reconstitution" that creates the potential for original productivity in the human language (Bronowski, 1977, p.147). The formal language, which can be used solely for analytic purposes, is seriously handicapped in its lack of reconstitutive power, a feature inherent in the natural language.

In fact, contrary to his formal language, man's natural language is cross-embedded with cognitive tools and apparatus which in sum, give him greater accommodating power and regulative capability. Taken alone, each of his cognitive tools embedded in the natural language may be imprecise and weak relative to the formal technique, but the natural language does permit man to apply a diversity of apparatus almost simultaneously, to allow a balanced set of tools to operate on a situation, to permit interfacings and interactions between these tools, which in turn provide better chances for the free play of man's creativity.

The weaknesses of man's natural language and the tools embedded therein are thus only apparent, and are true only when assessed on an item to item basis. Taken together, the capability of the natural language as a whole far outweighs the sum of its individual cognitive components, but unfortunately this is a point least understood. Similarly, other apparent weaknesses, such as multiple meanings, overtones and hidden ambiguities to the natural words and sentences, can in some cases turn out to be blessings. These ambiguities, etc. can be a fertile ground for the exploration and discovery of hidden likeness. Herein lies the unexpected links and conjunctions which provide the inventive ideas of science and knowledge (Bronowski, 1977, p.63).

The Superiority of the Natural Language

Even in the realm of the physical sciences, as Duhem pointed out (1904, pp.178-79), the statements of theoretical physics, just because they are more precise, are less certain, harder to confirm, than the vague statements of common sense. Wittgenstein too has rightly pointed out that ordinary language is frequently a better guide to the understanding of new and complex problems than are mathematical symbols, precisely because ordinary words are somewhat vague, general and capable of shifting their meaning and of embracing in a subtle way many of the more difficult issues that philosophy — or economics — confronts. Wittgenstein held that the illusion that for each word there exists a crystal-clear, sharply defined meaning creates the further illusion that because everyday language employs words and sentences that lack this crystal-clear language, it must be inadequate, or somehow, insufficient for the use of the serious thinker (Naess, 1968, pp.149-53).

Such a vagueness is inescapable, for man's natural language is not merely interwoven with a large part of his rational cognitive apparatus. Intimately interfaced with his perceptions, his intuitions and probably his unconscious, it also occupies a unique position in man's overall capacity to identify himself as a unique self and to make sense out of the external world. It is through this essential medium that all aspects of the extra-biological aspects of man tie and knit together meaningfully. Such a unique position and significance, needless to say, is denied of the formal language.[7]

Even in terms of rigor, a formalized system is not of necessity superior. We may perhaps need to distinguish here two meanings of rigor, the quantitative and the qualitative. While quantitative rigor is fully manifested in the formalized theory, qualitative rigor does not necessarily reside in the latter. It has a broader meaning and application. The qualitative rigor of a theory can be appraised in terms of the capability of its arguments in following through the most appropriate rules of logic and validity, its ability to free itself from conceptual incompatibilities and paradoxes, its ability to scan concepts from among competing versions, etc. As can be expected, qualitative rigor is manifestable in the qualitative formulation and precisification of coarse concepts and relations although it would be more difficult to gauge the degree of rigor and precisely measure it.

Even if social sciences have developed to the point where most of our knowledge can be encapsulated into the formal system, the superior role of the natural language remains unchallenged. The testing, the validation and falsification of a theoretical model are not merely mechanical processes whose outcome can be determined simply by logic. The result of testing or validation needs to be interpreted and in borderline cases, needs to be dealt with by expert judgement, case by case, for the standards by which a theory is to be judged cannot remain unchanged, but depend on the nature of the subject and its state of development.[8] Whether or not there is an adequate fit between data and model rests ultimately with the human judgement. Otherwise stated, the human factor in science cannot simply be ruled out.[9] And as long as this human factor plays an essential role, so remains his natural language where his judgements reside.

Indeed, there is ample new evidence showing that, contrary to the beliefs of Piaget and his colleagues, no cognitive system, whether human or artificial, can operate according to the laws of formal logic (Minsky, 1974). Formal logic is not a good description of how our mind usually works, or even how it should usually work. We do not think in terms of symbols and quasi-algebraic manipulations but in terms of words and meanings, for this is how we are shaped by million years of evolution.

Towards a Balanced View

Perhaps we can liken our natural language to our mind, and by contrast, the formal language is no more than a man-made machine, a powerful technique but only of limited applicability. The logic of the mind differs from formal logic in its ability to overcome and indeed to exploit the ambivalences of self-reference, so that they become the instruments of imagination (Bronowski,1977). In this same vein, Chomsky pointed out that human language should directly reflect the characteristics of human intellectual capacities and that (natural) language should be a direct "mirror of mind" (Chomsky, 1972, pp.ix-x).

The overall significance of the natural language is further reflected in the fact that even discourses on theoretical limits can be conducted in the natural language and that the natural language can capture with but little distortion the import of the formalized messages. According to Bridgman, there is in fact no sharp distinction between "mathematics" and "verbalizing" (Bridgman, 1961). An interesting example can be found in Hilbert's *Grundlagen der Geometrie* (1899) where he succeeded in producing a relative consistency proof for Euclidean Geometry entirely in ordinary language.[10] Indeed a post-empirical account of natural science today would include as an integral part of it that the language of natural science is irreducibly metaphorical and inexact, and formalizable only at the cost of distortion of the historical dynamics of scientific development and of the imaginative constructions in terms of which nature is interpreted by science (Hesse, 1980, p.173).

It is a big mistake, therefore, in the development of man's academic methodology to presume that the formal approach, which has proven beautifully to be of a great service to man in making up for part of his cognitive weaknesses, is capable of ultimately supplanting man's other cognitive potentials and strengths.[11] For this mistake, social sciences have paid a heavy price in terms of progress of knowledge.

A balanced view that emerges from this perspective is that it is not important whether or not an academic tool or method is natural or formal, qualitative or quantitative. Each particular tool has its role to play in promoting, exploiting and making up for man's cognitive strengths and weaknesses. "There is, for that matter, no intrinsic incompatibility between mathematics and literary sensibility" (Rosen, 1980, p.3). The important point, rather, is to understand their strengths and limitations and their relevance to application.[12] Any method, if it is to serve man well cognitively and academically, must be amenable to his natural cognitive potentials, and to shelter him from his cognitive pitfalls. Therein lies the true contribution and significance of the formal approach. Perhaps it is appropriate to repeat here Whitehead's statement on the value of proof: "Logic, conceived as an adequate analysis of the advance of thought, is a fake. It is a superb instrument, but it requires a background of common sense.... My point is the final outlook of philosophic thought cannot be based upon the exact statements which form the basis of special sciences. The exactness is a fake" (Whitehead, 1925).

NOTES

1. Mandler and Kesseu (1959) have pointed out the following undesirable qualities of the natural language, namely "universality" (the possibility of talking about everything — including language itself — in natural language giving rise to paradoxes and permitting confusion), "reification" (assumption that there is a nonverbal reality independent of the language), "vagueness" (indeterminacy of usage), "ambiguity" (different meanings for the same sentence in different contexts).

2. I am indebted to this latter term to Dr. Jonas Salk.

3. It has to be recognized that there is always an openness to concepts in science. The process of inquiry consists partly of employing concepts that are unclear, ambiguous, and sometimes even inconsistent; this is as true of "metascientific" concepts like 'observation', 'evidence', 'theory', 'confirmation', and 'explanation' as it is of concepts like 'mind', 'matter', 'element', 'particle', 'infinitesimal', 'force', 'energy', 'temperature', 'delta function', and 'singularity' at various states of scientific history. And beyond this is the openness and alterability of concepts however clear at any given stage ('life', 'electron', 'neutron', 'island', 'ocean', 'schizophrenia'). Greater clarification and closure are often achieved with further investigation (and we also learn in what clarification consists); but that clarification depends not only on "conceptual analysis," but also, and even primarily, on beliefs about the way the world is.... While it is the responsibility of philosophers of science to elucidate the general characteristics of scientific reasoning, we cannot expect some "absolute precision" (mythical in any case) in our analyses. What clarity we can achieve we must of course seek (and it is sometimes possible to be relatively clear about the respects in which clarity cannot be achieved); but we must be prepared to acknowledge irreducible vaguenesses, ambiguities, alternative interpretations, open possibilities of a variety of sorts (Shapere, 1984, p.219).

4. From G.L.S. Shackle in private correspondence.

5. This is congenial to what Mey called the "iceberg-model of knowledge." "To support something like ten percent explicit knowledge, which would commonly be considered genuine, requires ninety percent pre-requisite supporting knowledge, of a more covered or implicit nature" (Mey, 1982, p.19).

6. Once certain pre-formalized knowledge is being closed for formalization, such a route of knowledge production is being cut off.

7. "There cannot be a complete mathematizing of language or of 'sense', because mathematization studies formal structures, whereas there are fundamental senses of 'sense' that do not correspond to formal structures." See Rosen (1980, p.27).

8. See Ziman, (1978, p.36).

9. Compare Ziman (1978, p.99), "Science depends fundamentally on human powers of perception, recognition, discrimination and interpretation. The scientist as observer or communicator is an indispensable element of the knowledge system. But these powers have not been simulated by an artificial, non-human device: there is no computer program, no formal

algorithm, no string of logical operations, to which these processes are equivalent, or to which they can, in any practical sense, be reduced. Therefore — and this is one of the most important characteristics of the 'consensibility' model of science — scientific knowledge cannot be justified or validated by logic alone".

10. See Shand, (1980, p. 31).

11. In recognition of the limitation of economic model, Georgescu-Roegén has preferred to describe them as "analytic simile" (1971, p.332). Yet his conception that "an economic model is still exact even if it does not serve as a calculating device, provided that it constitutes a paper-and pencil representation of reality" (p.334) seems to contradict what we would expect of the conception of a simile.

12. "We must deplore the exaggerated fondness for mathematics which causes many to use that tool even when a simple diagram would suffice for the problem in its unadulterated form.... it would be utterly absurd to rely on ordinary logic alone whenever a mathematical tool can be used" (Georgescu-Roegén, 1971, pp.331-32).

BIBLIOGRAPHY

Ackermann, R. (1983) "Methodology and Economics," *Philosophical Forum*, 14:389-402.

Agassi, J. (1964) "The Nature of Scientific Problems and their Roots in Metaphysics," *The Critical Approach*, Bunge, M. ed., pp.189-211, Ill.: Glencoe.

⸻ (1971) "Tautology and Testability in Economics," *Philosophy of the Social Sciences*, 1:49-63.

⸻ and Cohen, R.S. eds. (1982) *Scientific Philosophy Today*, Dordrecht, Holland: D. Reidel.

Allais, M. (1977) "Theories of General Economic Equilibrium and Maximum Efficiency," *Equilibrium and Disequilibrium in Economic Theory*, Schwödiauer, G. ed., Dordrecht, Holland: D. Reidel.

Archard, D. (1984) *Consciousness and the Unconscious*, Hutchinson Publishing Group.

Archibald, G.C. (1959) "The State of Economic Science," *British Journal for the Philosophy of Science*, 10:58-69.

Arrow, K.J. (1951) "Mathematical Models in the Social Sciences," *The Policy Sciences*, Lerner, D. and Lasswell, H.D. eds., Stanford, Calif.: Stanford University Press, pp.129-54.

⸻ and Debreu, G. (1954) "Existence of an Equilibrium for a Competitive Economy," *Econometrica*, 22:265-90.

⸻ and Hahn, F.H. (1971) *General Competitive Analysis*, San Francisco: Holden-Day.

Bacharach, M. (1976) *Economics and the Theory of Games*, London: Macmillan.

Basemann, R.L. and Rhodes, G.F. Jr. eds., (1982-84) *Advances in Econometrics*, Vols. 1-3, Greenwich: JAI Press.

Bauer, P.T. (1981) *Equality, The Third World, and Economic Delusion*, Cambridge: Harvard University Press.

Benassy, J. (1982) *The Economics of Market Disequilibrium*, New York: Academic Press.

Blatt, J. (1983) "How Economists Misuse Mathematics," *Why Economics is not yet a Science*, Eichner, A.S. ed., New York: M.E. Sharpe.

Blaug, M. (1962) *Economic Theory in Retrospect*, 2nd ed. (1968) London: Heinemann.

⸻ (1973) *Ricardian Economics: A Historical Study*, Westport: Greenwood Press.

⸻ (1980) *The Methodology of Economics*, Cambridge: Cambridge University Press.

Bohm, D. (1980) *Wholeness and the Implicate Order,* London: Routledge & Kegan Paul.

Bohme, G. (1977) "Models for the Development of ·Science," *Science, Technology and Society,* Spiegel-Rösing, I. and de Solla Price, D. eds., London: Sage Publications.

Boulding, K.E. (1966) "The Economics of Knowledge and the Knowledge of Economics," *Economics of Information and Knowledge,* Lamberton, D.M. ed. (1971) Penguin Books.

_____ (1981) *Evolutionary Economics,* Beverly Hills: Sage Publications.

Bridgman, P.W. (1961) *The Nature of Thermodynamics,* New York.

Bronowski, J. (1966) "The Logic of the Mind," *The American Scholar,* Vol. 35, 2: 233-42.

_____ (1967) *Human and Animal Languages to Honor Roman Jakobson,* Vol. 1, pp.374-95, The Haque, Mouton & Co.

_____ (1977) *A Sense of the Future,* Ariotti, P.E. ed., Cambridge, Mass.: MIT Press.

_____ (1978) *The Origins of Knowledge and Imagination,* Yale University Press.

Brown, J.A.C. (1961) *Freud and the Post-Freudians,* Penguin Books.

Caldwell, B. (1982) *"Beyond Positivism,"* Economic Methodology in the *Twentieth Century,* London: Allen & Unwin.

_____ ed. (1984) *Appraisal and Criticism in Economics,* London: Allen & Unwin.

Canterbery, E.R. (1976) *The Making of Economics,* 2nd ed. (1980) Belmont: Wadworth.

Chomsky, N. (1968) *Language and Mind,* enlarged ed. (1972) Harcourt Brace Jovanovich.

_____ (1975) *Reflections on Language,* New York: Pantheon.

_____ (1980) "Rules and Representations," *The Behavioral and Brain Sciences,* 3:1-61.

Church, A. (1956) *Introduction to Mathematical Logic,* Vol. 1, Princeton, NJ: Princeton University Press.

Churchland, P.M. (1979) *Scientific Realism and the Plasticity of Mind,* Cambridge: Cambridge University Press.

_____ and Hooker, C.A. eds. (1985) *Images of Science,* Chicago: University of Chicago Press.

Cohen, R.S. and Wartofsky, M.W. eds. (1983) *Epistemology, Methodology, and the Social Sciences,* Dordrecht, Holland: D. Reidel.

Conant, J.B. (1951) *Science and Common Sense,* New Haven: Yale University Press.

Coombs, C.H. (1983) *Psychology and Mathematics — An Essay on Theory,* University of Michigan Press.

Craig, W. (1953) "On Axiomatizability within a System," *Journal of Symbolic Logic,* 18:30-32.

Crane, D. (1972) *Invisible Colleges,* Chicago: University of Chicago Press.

Crook, J.H. (1980) *The Evolution of Human Consciousness,* Oxford: Clarendon Press.

Deane, P. (1978) *The Evolution of Economic Ideas,* Cambridge: Cambridge University Press.

Debreu, G. (1959) "The Theory of Value: An Axiomatic Analysis of Economic Equilibrium," *Cowles Foundation Monograph,* No. 17, New York: John Wiley.

——— (1983) *Mathematical Economics: Twenty Papers of Gerard Debreu,* Cambridge: Cambridge University Press.

——— (1985) Frisch Memorial Lecture delivered at the Fifth World Congress of the Econometric Society held at MIT.

Dobb, M. (1973) *Theories of Value and Distribution since Adam Smith,* Cambridge: Cambridge University Press.

Duhem, P. (1904) "La theorie physique: son objet, sa structure" page references to *The Aim and Structure of Physical Theory,* tr. Wiener from the 2nd edition (1914) (Atheneum 1962).

Earl, P.E. (1983) *The Economic Imagination,* New York: M.E. Sharpe.

Eichner, A.S. ed. (1983) *Why Economics is not yet a Science,* New York: M.E. Sharpe.

Faust, D. (1984) *The Limits of Scientific Reasoning,* Minnesota: University of Minnesota Press.

Fodor, J.A. (1983) *The Modularity of Mind,* Cambridge, Mass.: MIT Press.

Friedman, M. (1953) *Essays in Positive Economics,* Chicago: University of Chicago Press.

Frisch, R. (1970) *Induction, Growth and Trade, Essays in Honour of Sir Roy Harrod,* Eltis, W.A., Scott, M.F. and Wolfe, J.N. eds.

Fromm, E. (1941) *Escape from Freedom,* New York: Farrar and Rinehart.

Gale, D. (1955) "The Law of Supply and Demand," *Mathematica Scandinavica*, 3:87-101.

Georgescu-Roegen, N. (1971) *The Entropy Law and the Economic Process*, Cambridge: Harvard University Press.

_____ (1979) "Methods in Economic Science," *Journal of Economic Issues*, 13:317-28.

Granger, G-G (1983) *Formal Thought and the Sciences of Man*, Dordrecht, Holland: D. Reidel.

Gödel, K. (1962) *On Formally Undecidable Propositions*, New York: Basic Books.

Goffman, W. (1971) "A Mathematical Model for Analyzing the Growth of a Scientific Discipline," *Journal Association Computing Machinery*, 18:173-85.

Griliches, Z. and Intriligator, M.D. (1983-84) *Handbook of Econometrics*, Vol. 1, Amsterdam: North Holland.

Hahn, F.H. (1973) *On the Notion of Equilibrium in Economics. An Inaugural Lecture*, Cambridge: Cambridge University Press.

_____ (1973) "The Winter of our Discontent," *Economica*, 40:322-30.

Hausman, D.M. ed. (1985) *The Philosophy of Economics — An Anthology*, Cambridge: Cambridge University Press.

Hayek, F.A. (1967) *Studies in Philosophy, Politics and Economics*, London: Routledge & Kegan Paul.

_____ (1978) *New Studies in Philosophy, Politics, Economics, and the History of Ideas*, London: Routledge & Kegan Paul.

Hempel, C.G. (1977) "Formulation and Formalization of Scientific Theories," *The Structure of Scientific Theories*, Suppe, F. ed., 2nd ed., Urbana: University of Illinois Press.

Henkin, L., Suppes, P. and Tarski, A. eds. (1959) *The Axiomatic Method with Special Reference to Geometry and Physics*, Amsterdam: North Holland.

Hesse, M. (1974) *The Structure of Scientific Inference*, Berkeley: University of California Press.

_____ (1980) *Revolution and Reconstruction in the Philosophy of Science*, The Harvester Press.

Hicks, J.R. (1939) *Value and Capital*, Oxford: Oxford University Press.

Hollis, M. and Nell, E.J. (1975) *Rational Economic Man: A Philosophical Critique of Neo-Classical Economics*, Cambridge: Cambridge University Press.

Holton, G. (1973) *Thematic Origins of Scientific Thought: Kepler to Einstein*, Cambridge: Harvard University Press.

_____ (1978) *The Scientific Imagination: Case Studies,* Cambridge: Cambridge University Press.

_____ (1981) "Thematic Presuppositions and the Direction of Scientific Advance," *Scientific Explanation,* Heath, A.F. ed., New York: Oxford University Press.

Hutchison, T.W. (1977) *Knowledge and Ignorance in Economics,* Oxford: Basil Blackwell.

_____ (1978) *On Revolutions and Progress in Economic Knowledge,* Cambridge: Cambridge University Press.

Iwai, K. (1981) *Disequilibrium Dynamics, A Theoretical Analysis of Inflation and Unemployment,* New Haven: Yale University Press.

Jaynes, J. (1976) *The Origin of Consciousness in the Breakdown of the Bicameral Mind,* Boston: Houghton-Mifflin.

Johnson-Laird, P.N. (1983) *Mental Models,* Cambridge, Mass.: Harvard University Press.

Kaldor, N. (1972) "The Irrelevance of Equilibrium Economics," *Economic Journal,* 82(328):1237-55.

Kamarck, A.M. (1983) *Economics and the Real World,* U.K.: Basil Blackwell.

Katouzian, H. (1980) *Ideology and Method in Economics,* New York: New York University Press.

Katzner, D.W. (1983) *Analysis without Measurement,* Cambridge: Cambridge University Press.

Klamer, A. (1983) *Conversations with Economists,* New Jersey: Rowman & Allanheld.

Klant, J.J. (1984) *The Rules of the Game,* Swart, I. tr., Cambridge: Cambridge University Press.

Kleene, S.C. (1952) *Introduction to Metamathematics,* Amsterdam: North Holland.

Kline, M. (1980) *Mathematics — The Loss of Certainty,* Oxford University Press.

Koopmans, T.C. (1957) *Three Essays on the State of Economic Science,* McGraw-Hill.

Kornai, J. (1971) *Anti-Equilibrium: On Economic Systems Theory and the Tasks of Research,* Amsterdam: North Holland.

Krajewski, W. ed. (1982) *Polish Essays in the Philosophy of the Natural Sciences,* Dordrecht, Holland: D. Reidel.

Kuhn, T.S. (1962) *The Structure of Scientific Revolutions,* enlarged ed.,(1970), Chicago: University of Chicago Press.

_____ (1977) *The Essential Tension: Selected Studies in Scientific Tradition and Change,* Chicago & London: University of Chicago Press.

Kyburg, H.E. Jr. (1968) *Philosophy of Science: A Formal Approach,* New York: Macmillan.

Lakatos, I. (1976) *Proofs and Refutations. The Logic of Mathematical Discovery,* Cambridge: Cambridge University Press.

_____ (1978) *The Methodology of Scientific Research Programmes. Philosophical Papers,* Worrall, J. and Currie, G. eds. Vols. 1-2, Cambridge: Cambridge University Press.

_____ and Musgrave, A. eds. (1970) *Criticism and the Growth of Knowledge,* Cambridge: Cambridge University Press.

Latsis, S.J. ed. (1976) *Method and Appraisal in Economics,* Cambridge: Cambridge University Press.

Leibenstein, H. (1950) "Bandwagon, Snob and Veblen Effects in the Theory of Consumer's Demand," *Quarterly Journal of Economics,* May 1950.

Leontief, W. (1971) "Theoretical Assumptions and Nonobserved Facts," Presidential Address to American Economic Association, 29 Dec. 1970, *American Economic Review,* 61(1):1-7.

Loasby, B.J. (1976) *Choice, Complexity and Ignorance,* Cambridge: Cambridge University Press.

Lutz, M.A. and Lux, K. (1979) *The Challenge of Humanistic Economics,* The Benjamin/Cummings Publishing Company, Inc.

Machlup, F. (1978) *Methodology of Economics and Other Social Sciences,* New York: Academic Press.

Madden, E.H. ed. (1960) *The Structure of Scientific Thought,* Boston, Mass.: Houghton Mifflin.

Makarov, V.L. (1976) "Economic Equilibrium Model with Innovations," *Optimization,* N 18, 1976, Proceedings of the Institute of Mathematics, Siberian Branch of the Acad. Sci. U.S.S.R.

Mandler, G. and Kessen, W. (1959) *The Language of Psychology,* New York: Wiley.

McCloskey, D.N. (1985) *The Rhetoric of Economics,* University of Wisconsin Press (proof copy).

McKenzie, L.W. (1954) "On Equilibrium in Graham's Model of World Trade and Other Competitive Systems," *Econometrica,* 22.

Mckinsey, J.C.C., Sugar, A. and Suppes, P. (1953) "Axiomatic Foundations of Classical Particle Mechanics," *Journal of Rational Mechanics and Analysis,* 2:253-72.

Meehan, E.J. (1982) *Economics and Policymaking — The Tragic Illusion,* U.K.: Greenwood Press.

Melitz, J. (1965) "Friedman and Machlup on the Significance of Testing Economic Assumptions," *Journal of Political Economy,* 73:37-60.

Metzler, L.A. (1945) "Stability of Multiple Markets: The Hicks Conditions," *Econometrica,* 13:277-92.

Mey, M.D. (1982) *The Cognitive Paradigm,* Dordrecht, Holland: D. Reidel.

Minsky, M.L. (1974) "A Framework of Representing Knowledge," Cambridge, Mass.: MIT Artificial Intelligence Laboratory. Artificial Intelligence Memo No. 306.

———— (1977) "Plain Talk about Neurodevelopmental Epistemology," Cambridge, Mass.: MIT Artificial Intelligence Laboratory. Artificial Intelligence Memo No. 430.

Mises, L.v. (1966) *Human Action: A Treatise on Economics,* 3rd ed., New York: Henry Regnery.

Morishima, M. (1984) "The Good and Bad Use of Mathematics," *Economics in Disarray,* Wiles, P. and Routh, G. eds., Oxford: Basil Blackwell.

Mulchkhuyse, J. (1960) *Molecules and Models: Investigations on the Axiomatization of Structure Theory in Chemistry,* Thesis, Amsterdam: North Holland.

Mulkay, M.J., Gilbert, G.N. and Woolgar, S., (1975) "Problem Areas and Research Networks in Science," *Sociology,* 9:187-203.

Mullins, N.C. (1973) *Theories and Theory Groups in Contemporary American Sociology,* New York: Harper and Row.

———— (1973) *Science: Some Sociological Perspectives,* Indianapolis & New York: Bobbs-Merrill.

Naess, A. (1968) *Four Modern Philosophers,* Chicago.

Nash, J.F. (1953) "Two-person Cooperative Games," *Econometrica, 21:128.*

Nelson, R.R. and Winter, S.G. (1982) *An Evolutionary Theory of Economic Change,* The Belknap Press of Harvard University Press.

Neumann, J.v. (1937) "A Model of General Economic Equilibrium," Morgenstern, O. tr., *Review of Economic Studies,* 13(1945-46):1-9.

———— and Morgenstern, O. (1944) *Theory of Games and Economic Behavior,* Princeton: Princeton University Press.

Nickles, T. ed. (1980) *Scientific Discovery, Logic, and Rationality,* Dordrecht, Holland: D. Reidel.

Nicolis, G. and Prigogine, I. (1977) *Self-organization in Nonequilibrium Systems: From Dissipative Structures to Order Through Fluctuations,* New York: Wiley — Interscience.

O'Driscoll, G.P. Jr. and Rizzo, M.J. (1985) *The Economics of Time and Ignorance,* U.K.: Basil Blackwell.

Pandit, G.L. (1983) *The Structure and Growth of Scientific Knowledge,* Dordrecht, Holland: D. Reidel.

Pankow, W. (1976) "Openness as Self-transcendence," *Evolution and Consciousness: Human Systems in Transition,* Jantsch and Waddinton eds., Reading, Mass.: Addison-Wesley.

Pasinetti, L.K. (1981) *Structural Change and Economic Growth — A Theoretical Essay on the Dynamics of the Wealth of Nations,* Cambridge: Cambridge University Press.

Phelps Brown, E.H. (1972) "The Underdevelopment of Economics," *Economic Journal,* 82:1-10.

Piaget, J. (1952) *The Origins of Intelligence in Children,* Cook, M. tr., New York: International University Press.

_____ (1970) *Genetic Epistemology,* Duckworth, E. tr., New York: Columbia University Press.

Pomper, P. (1985) *The Structure of Mind in History,* New York: Columbia University Press.

Popper, K.R. (1957) *The Poverty of Historicism,* corrected ed. (1961) London: Routledge & Kegan Paul.

_____ (1959) *The Logic of Scientific Discovery,* reprinted (1965), New York: Harper Torchbooks.

_____ (1963) *Conjectures and Refutations. The Growth of Scientific Knowledge,* London: Routledge & Kegan Paul.

_____ (1972) *Objective Knowledge: An Evolutionary Approach,* London: Oxford University Press.

_____ (1982) *The Open Universe,* London: Hutchison.

Prigogine, I. (1984) *Order out of Chaos: Man's New Dialogue with Nature,* Bantam Books.

Radnitzky, G. (1973) "Towards a Theory of Traditions in Science," *Communication and Cognition,* 6:15-46.
_____ and Anderson, G. eds. (1979) *The Structure and Development of Science,* Dordrecht, Holland: D. Reidel.
Ramsey, F.P. (1931) *The Foundations of Mathematics and Other Logical Essays,* London: Kegan Paul.
Robbins, L. (1932) *An Essay on the Nature and Significance of Economic Science,* London: Macmillan.
Robinson, J. (1933) *The Economics of Imperfect Competition,* Macmillan.
_____ (1962) *Economic Philosophy,* C.A. Watts.
Rosen, S. (1980) *The Limits of Analysis,* New Haven: Yale University Press.
Rosenbleuth, W. and Wiener, N. (1945) "The Role of Models in Science," *Philosophy of Science,* 12:318-21.
Routh, G. (1975) *The Origin of Economic Ideas,* Macmillan Press.

Salmon, W.C. (1984) *Scientific Explanation and the Causal Structure of the World,* New Jersey: Princeton University Press.
Samuelson, P.A. (1941) "Linear and Non-Linear Systems," *Econometrica,* 10:1-25.
_____ (1941) "The Stability of Equilibrium Comparative Statics and Dynamics," *Econometrica,* 9:97-120.
_____ (1947) *Foundation of Economic Analysis,* Cambridge: Harvard University Press.
Schwodiauer, G. ed. (1978) *Equilibrium and Disequilibrium in Economic Theory,* Dordrecht, Holland: D. Reidel.
Seltman, M. and Seltman, P. (1985) *Piaget's Logic — A Critique of Genetic Epistemology,* London: George Allen & Unwin.
Shackle, G.S.L. (1972) *Epistemics and Economics: A Critique of Economic Doctrines,* Cambridge: Cambridge University Press.
Shand, A.H. (1980) *Subjectivist Economics: The New Austrian School,* The Pica Press.
Shapere, D. (1974) *Discovery, Rationality, and Progress in Science: A Perspective in the Philosophy of Science,* Schaffner and Cohen.
_____ (1984) *Reason and the Search for Knowledge,* Dordrecht, Holland: D. Reidel.
Simon, H.A. (1977) *Models of Discovery and Other Topics in the Methods of Science,* Vol. 54, *Boston Studies in the Philosophy of Science,* Dordrecht, Holland: D. Reidel.

Skolem, T. (1955) *Mathematical Interpretation of Formal Systems,* Amsterdam: North Holland.

_____ (1970) *Selected Works in Logic,* Fenstad, J.E. ed., Oslo, Universitets-forlaget.

Smithies, A. (1942) "The Stability of Competitive Equilibrium," *Econometrica,* 10:256-57.

Stahl, I. (1977) "An n-person Bargaining Game in the Extensive Form," *Mathematical Economics and Game Theory,* Henn, R. and Moeschlin, O. eds., Springer.

Stewart, I.M.T. (1979) *Reasoning and Method in Economics: An Introduction to Economic Methodology,* London: McGraw-Hill.

Suppe, F. ed. (1977) *The Structure of Scientific Theories,* 2nd ed., Urbana: University of Illinois Press.

Suppes, P. (1968) "The Desirability of Formalization in Science," *Journal of Philosophy,* 65:651-64.

_____ (1969) *Studies in the Methodology and Foundations of Science,* Dordrecht, Holland: D. Reidel.

Tarski, A. (1956) *Logic, Semantics, Metamathematics,* Woodger, J.H. tr., Oxford: Clarendon Press.

Telser, L. (1972) *Competition, Collusion, and Game Theory,* Chicago: Aldine.

Thurow, L.C. (1983) *Dangerous Currents — The State of Economics,* New York: Random House.

Tinbergen, J. and Bos, H.C. (1962) *Mathematical Models of Economic Growth,* New York: McGraw-Hill.

Toulmin, S. (1967) "The Evolutionary Development of Natural Science," *American Scientist,* 55:456-71.

_____ (1972) *Human Understanding,* Vol. 1, *The Collective Use and Evolution of Concepts,* Princeton: Princeton University Press.

_____ (1977) "Postscript: The Structure of Scientific Theories," *The Structure of Scientific Theories,* Suppe, F. ed., 2nd ed., Urbana: University of Illinois Press.

Turing, A.M. (1936) "On Computable Numbers with an Application to the Entscheidungs Problem," *Proceedings of the London Mathematical Society,* Series 2, 42:230-65.

_____ (1950) "Computing Machinery and Intelligence," *Mind,* 59:433-60.

Van Frassen, B.C. (1980) *The Scientific Image,* Oxford: Clarendon Press.

Veblen, T. (1899) *The Theory of the Leisure Class* (1931) New York: Viking Press.

Walters, A.A. (1963) "Production and Cost Functions: An Econometric Survey," *Econometrica,* 31:1-66.

Ward, B. (1972) *What's Wrong with Economics?* London: Macmillan.

Warsh, D. (1984) *The Idea of Economic Complexity,* New York: The Viking Press.

Watkin, J. (1978) "The Popperian Approach to Scientific Knowledge", *Progress and Rationality in Science,* Radnitzky, G. and Anderson, G. eds., pp.23-43.

Weimer, W.B. (1974) "The History of Psychology and its Retrieval from Historiography: II. Some Lessons for the Methodology of Scientific Research," *Science Studies,* 4:367-96.

Weintraub, E.R. (1977) "General Equilibrium Theory," *Modern Economic Thought,* Weintraub. S. ed., Oxford: Basil Blackwell.

———— (1985) *General Equilibrium Analysis — Studies in Appraisal,* Cambridge: Cambridge University Press. (Proof Copy)

Weiss, P. (1960) "Knowledge: A Growth Process," reprinted in *The Growth of Knowledge,* Kochen, M. ed. (1967) New York: Wiley.

Wiles, P. and Routh, G. eds. (1984) *Economics in Disarray,* Oxford: Basil Blackwell.

Wiseman, J. ed. (1983) *Beyond Positive Economics? — Proceedings of Section F (Economics) of the British Association for the Advancement of Science, York 1981,* London and Basingstoke: Macmillan.

Wittgenstein, L. (1953) *Philosophical Investigations,* Anscombe, G. and Rhees, R. eds., Anscombe, G. tr., Oxford: Basil Blackwell.

Woo, H.K.H. (1984) *The Unseen Dimensions of Wealth,* Calif.: Victoria Press.

Woodger, J.H. (1937) *The Axiomatic Method in Biology,* Cambridge: Cambridge University Press.

Worswick, G.D.N. (1972) "Is Progress in Economic Science Possible?" Presidential Address to Section F of the British Association, 2 Sept. 1971, *Economic Journal,* 82(325):73-86.

Ziman, J. (1978) *Reliable Knowledge: An Exploration of the Grounds for Belief in Science,* London: Cambridge University Press.